AF184116

Family Governance and Surplus Wealth

Sustaining Family Fortunes

Russell Prior

Globe Law and Business

Author
Russell Prior

Managing director
Sian O'Neill

Family Governance and Surplus Wealth: Sustaining Family Fortunes
is published by

Globe Law and Business Ltd
3 Mylor Close
Horsell
Woking
Surrey GU21 4DD
United Kingdom
Tel: +44 20 3745 4770
www.globelawandbusiness.com

Family Governance and Surplus Wealth: Sustaining Family Fortunes

ISBN 9781787424869
EPUB ISBN 9781787424876
Adobe PDF ISBN 9781787424883
Mobi ISBN 9781787424890

Table of contents

Dedication
For Samuel and Joshua

The truly fortunate person has created his own good fortune through good habits of the soul, good intentions and good actions.
Marcus Aurelius

All fortune is good fortune; for it either rewards, disciplines, amends or punishes, and so is either useful or just.
Boethius, *The Consolation of Philosophy*

Acknowledgements

I would like to acknowledge the hundreds of business owners, wealthy individuals and members of their families who have shared their intensely private thoughts on surplus wealth with me. It has been a privilege to have had access to the hopes, fears and anxieties that people harbour, knowing that there are very few with whom they can share their feelings, let alone feel able to go to for help or advice. Without them this book would not have been possible.

In addition, I would like to thank my family and the friends and colleagues with whom I have worked, who have listened to my pontifications and endless stories as I tried to make sense of what I've heard.

Special thanks, of course, to those who have reviewed my work – Stephen, Sophie, Carly, Patrick, Komal, Paul and Nadine.

And finally, my thanks to those closest to me who have supported me in achieving something I never thought I had within me.

Part I:
The challenges
of surplus wealth

1. Introduction

This book deals with the challenges that come from possessing a family fortune. It doesn't matter whether this wealth was generated by you, received by way of gift or inheritance, or won on a lottery.

A fortune presents opportunities and challenges, and a system is required in order to understand both – and to manage them sensibly.

This matters because we know that for many families their fortunes, far from bringing happiness, can cause misfortune. It matters because the issues and choices that face people dealing with a fortune are not only unavoidable but very different from those that face the overwhelming majority of the population.

Most who find themselves in this position are deeply unprepared. It can be a lonely place with little support, even from those closest to them. There are many stories in the public realm – sadly often sensationalist and portraying only the negative – about what happens to families with a fortune behind them. It may only be many years later, having learned some harsh lessons on the way, that they come to terms with their supposedly good fortune.

Throughout this book I will use the term 'surplus wealth' rather than 'fortune', so as to remove any connotations of chance or luck and to enable us to think in terms of surplus wealth as being something that can be systematically managed.

Even the term 'surplus wealth' comes with a caveat – we need to balance the focus on financial wealth with a focus on the importance of non-financial wealth. That is why I appreciate the sentiments contained in the two quotes at the beginning of the book. Good habits, good intentions and good actions can create and maintain good fortune; but we know from the many stories of those in possession of a fortune that it can be punishing as well as rewarding.

This book, then, aims to set out how the issues arising from having surplus wealth can be dealt with in an orderly way by developing and maintaining a system of family governance. In this context, the aim of governance is to increase the chances that surplus wealth will enhance your life and the lives of those around you rather than having a detrimental effect.

2. Surplus wealth

Surplus wealth, quite simply, is a level of wealth beyond that which can be consumed during one's lifetime.[1]

We can't put a figure on the level at which surplus wealth starts as it will vary between people according to two obvious factors:

- how long a person will live; and
- their lifestyle or wealth consumption rate.

Equally, the surplus wealth threshold needs to be exceeded by quite some margin for there to be a meaningful surplus that requires management. Whereas the majority of the population is worried about having enough money to survive – whether for a day, a week, a year or the rest of their lives – those with surplus wealth shouldn't have to think, let alone worry, about this.

The number of people falling into this category is very small. In even the wealthiest economies the percentage of the population that might be regarded as having surplus wealth is tiny. In the US, for example, we are talking about somewhere between 0.03% and 0.07% of the population.[2]

The numbers appear to be growing, however. The total number of ultra-high net worth individuals (UHNWIs)[3] in the world is now estimated at just over 513,000,[4] an increase of 6.4% in the 12 months to January 2020. While the US currently dominates, with just under 50% of the total, strong future growth is to be found elsewhere. India is forecast to grow its UHNWI population by 73% over the next five years; China by 57.6%; and even the UK by 31%.

If we take a look at the split between inherited and self-made fortunes we can get a feel for the level of preparedness within these families. Those families who encounter surplus wealth for the first time are, by definition, likely to be less prepared for its effects, although a fortune generated by previous generations is no guarantee of success.

One report suggests that 67.7% of the ultra-wealthy around the globe are self-made,[5] with only 8.5% deemed to have gained their wealth purely from an inheritance. The balance of 23.7% became wealthy through a combination of both.

But this simplistic view doesn't show the effects of some other interesting underlying influences. Family background, culture, upbringing and values have a significant role to play in beliefs, attitudes and behaviours regarding wealth, and a greater focus on the non-financial elements of wealth can act as a counterbalance to surplus financial wealth. Non-financial wealth includes things such as:

- physical, mental, spiritual and emotional wellbeing;
- reputation and social capital;
- values and principles;
- history, traditions and rituals;
- family education;
- family communication and decision making;
- family relationships; and
- legacy.

Viewed from the perspective of normal levels of wealth, it takes a moment or two to understand why having to deal with serious surplus wealth matters. Most people, when offered the prospect of having more money than they need, instantly see it as removing any worries they might have in their life. After all, why do so many people play lotteries? I accept that most don't expect to win, but that's not the same as saying they don't want to win. Of course they do. They would love to find themselves in a position where they believe they won't have to worry about money.

Yet we know that surplus wealth can be corrosive and is no guarantee of happiness – clogs to clogs in three generations, as the saying goes. And look at the stories of how fortunes have destroyed individuals and relationships within families. I put this down to three main factors:

- **A misunderstanding of the dynamics of surplus wealth:** Often there is a misplaced focus of activity when surplus wealth is encountered. At one end of the spectrum we see individuals launching into a spending spree. At the other we see an obsessive, fear-driven focus on protecting the money and keeping it secret. A quick look at the contrasting marketing and sales pitches of, on the one hand, the luxury goods industry, and on the other, the trust and estate planning and investment management industries, shows how easy it is to be sucked into either of these.
- **The trap of what I call 'money without purpose':** Idle or wild spending, consuming, giving or donating money rarely generate a sense of purpose. In fact embarking on such a spree, whatever the focus, can severely damage what sense of purpose there was before the surplus wealth arrived. Without being guided by a pre-existing or pre-developed sense of purpose these things are much more likely to end up generating, in due course, feelings of frustration, disappointment, regret and even waste. Which can then turn into even more destructive behaviours.
- **Family dynamics and family culture, comprising three elements:**
    - The generators of the surplus wealth will have their own individual backgrounds and culture, built up within the history of their separate families.
    - They will have developed a joint, shared way of doing things in creating their surplus wealth.
    - There will be the family culture within which they have been brought up and raised their own children.

    This complex historical family culture jigsaw is unlikely to have been planned proactively; it will just have evolved. And the surplus wealth lands on top of it.

I'll share two examples that highlight these factors:

- On meeting a multi-billionaire from a newly emerging economy we were engaged in a discussion about why he wanted much of the surplus wealth he had created to be dedicated to philanthropy. He contrasted the economic and political development path of his country with that of mine, the United Kingdom. "Philanthropy and charitable giving," he said thoughtfully, "are part of the system in your country that provides you with the values you have. My country doesn't have that system, that history, those values. I want to use philanthropy not only to do good in my country, but also to help define my family's values."

- A more regular occurrence is what often happens when I meet couples for the first time to talk to them about the purpose of their surplus wealth. As I ask each to explain their motivations and their view of the purpose for their surplus wealth I find, unsurprisingly, quite a high degree of overlap. What's interesting, however, is the number of couples who are surprised by what they don't know about each other's thinking. I often hear, "You've never told me that" or "I didn't know you thought that", alongside slightly bewildered faces, as they look at each other trying to understand why this is new news.

The simple fact is that it's hard to prepare for the effect of surplus wealth.

Yet, standing back, there's a relatively straightforward process to bring order and purpose to surplus wealth. It requires, first, a calculation of the level of core wealth appropriate specifically to you – what you need for the rest of your life. Anything above this is surplus wealth. And secondly, it requires the development of a purpose and strategy for the surplus wealth. What is the point of the wealth and what is it going to be used for? I use the term 'wealth philosophy' to describe this purpose and strategy. It should provide the guiding principles for the family in relation to their surplus wealth and a narrative that links the family history and culture with the future.

The purpose and strategy should also describe the roles that family members will have in relation to the surplus wealth, whether as stewards, beneficiaries or managers, or even generators of greater wealth.

"What is the point of the wealth and what is it going to be used for? I use the term 'wealth philosophy' to describe this purpose and strategy. It should provide the guiding principles for the family in relation to their surplus wealth and a narrative that links the family history and culture with the future."

And finally there should be a plan and processes for the purposeful management of the surplus wealth.

The core wealth calculation – what is needed to maintain your lifestyle for the rest of your life – needs to look at income generation on the one hand and expenditure on the other, and to identify possible risks. This calculation can take into account whatever level of lifestyle is desired; the point is to include such expenditure in the core wealth calculation, not in the surplus wealth calculation.

While surplus wealth is anything above what's needed for the rest of your life, it should be borne in mind that the number of years of life you have ahead of you will be a major driver of the level of core wealth you need. In making the calculation, prudence would suggest planning and allowing for a long life and a range of eventualities that may occur over such a period.

With the level of surplus wealth identified, determining what to do with it is rather more straightforward than many suppose. The simple truth is that surplus wealth can only be used in three ways:

- by attempting to consume it;[6]
- by sharing the wealth with family and friends; and/or
- by giving it away in the form of philanthropy.

And while doing any or all of these can be deferred, they can't be put off indefinitely. Death, I'm afraid, will eventually force the issue. And a premature death will just increase the level of surplus wealth to be dealt with.

The relatively simple list of things that can be done with surplus wealth doesn't necessarily make it easy to determine what to do or help to identify the balance between them. But what it does allow, in my experience, is for people to approach the issue with much, much greater focus. Simplifying things puts time on their side and should allow a sensible approach and plan to be put in place.

3. The human face of wealth

Bringing purpose and focus to the application of surplus wealth is an intensely personal process. A big part of the answer to what to do will lie deep in ones beliefs, attitudes and behaviours in terms of money, family, friends and society at large. It will be a function of your experiences, too, and how those around you have behaved in relation to money. It might be influenced by culture or your religious beliefs.

Done well, the answer should be driven by a balanced sense of the good that you would like to come from the wealth, and an avoidance of harm that can be created by it. Importantly, it should prompt thoughts regarding the obligations and responsibilities that come with wealth, whereas many just think of the rights and opportunities.

And crucially, we need to recognise that surplus wealth causes problems for more than just you. It affects partners, spouses, children and the wider family. What might seem simple and positive in your mind may not be seen in the same way by those close to you who create their own expectations and reactions – and that's before you make any decisions. So we really need to think through the consequences, intended and unintended.

As we think about what to do with surplus wealth, as we begin to articulate vision, goals and objectives, we will begin to experience dilemmas, contradictions and emotions. And of course as we project these onto the potential beneficiaries of this surplus wealth, we can expose the inconsistencies in, or even hypocrisy of, our own behaviours and attitudes to money. There follow one or two examples of the sorts of things that crop up.

3.1 Fairness vs meritocracy

A trait of many of the parents with surplus wealth that I meet is the desire to treat their children fairly, which often translates into equally. Nothing wrong with that. Except, perhaps, when situations arise where it's not possible. A classic case is the appointment of the next family head or CEO of the family business. A choice may need to be made between children or cousins. Merit should be the driver here, not fairness, but families often struggle with this. And this is amplified greatly when it comes to the question of what to do as regards future ownership.

Another situation arises where children within a family have taken very different paths and generated different levels of wealth or success for themselves. Should parents treat the children equally, or is it fairer to weight the help towards those with less?

3.2 Encouragement of virtue vs punishment of waywardness

Unfortunately, wealth is sometimes used as a tool to encourage certain behaviours or outcomes. While the beneficiaries of the rewards might feel good, care needs to be taken that those not receiving don't feel punished or alienated. This can be seen by some members of the next generation as favouritism, and can drive a wedge between family members.

3.3 Control and conditionality (or 'ruling from the grave')

Another strong trait is the desire of some in the senior generation to maintain control, often even beyond their lifetime. With such a strong internal, almost egotistical, focus, rarely is the impact on the next generation considered, let alone understood. So what happens in most of these scenarios? The next generation rebel, even if silently, and will often end up doing almost the opposite of the parents' wishes.

Milder versions of this trait might extend to the placing of age limits on access to wealth or using structures and advisers or professionals to protect the wealth from children and young adults. Worse, sometimes even outsourcing to advisers the task of communicating these controls or limits to one's own children. Sadly, these actions often have the effect of preventing the children from learning, becoming prepared or gaining experience in what they will need in later life. And being treated like that by their own parents doesn't bode well for future relationships.

And because so much of what children learn is from watching what their parents do, these behaviours can become embedded in the way they, in turn, behave towards their own children.

3.4 Secrecy driven by the fear of harm
Secrecy, or protecting the next generation from knowledge about the level of surplus wealth, is another fairly common approach. The justification is usually a fear that knowledge of the wealth will cause the children to lose all sense of drive and aspiration for themselves. Again, the unintended consequence is that the family does little to prepare the next generation for when the wealth eventually comes, and that's without the negative feelings felt by the next generation about why their parents didn't inform them or trust them when they were younger.

3.5 Passing on nothing, giving it all away
And I still occasionally encounter families who want to pass nothing (or very little) to their children – their intention is to give it all away. Their children have to make their own way.

In the scenarios I encounter, the views are nearly always resolutely held. We must remind ourselves why and how such beliefs and attitudes are formed, and what causes the behaviours we see. And we should be prepared to have a discussion with, and to challenge, the owners of the surplus wealth as to why they hold the views they do.

It's not about agreeing with or opposing their views, or trying to impose our own. Rather, we should help them to articulate the rationale for and consequences of their beliefs, attitudes and behaviours, and help them to see – particularly from their perspective – some of the unintended consequences. We should help them to appreciate that being able to explain their perspective will help the next generation to understand what they're thinking, instead of being hit with a wall of silence or an unyielding set of views. And we should help them to see that the creation of a purpose for their wealth, one that is shared with those it will affect, is likely to significantly improve the chances of their goals and objectives being fulfilled.

Yet what we see with many of the examples I've outlined above is parents reverting to an adult/child approach to the next generation, even if the next generation are well into their adult lives, probably with families of their own. And their approach to the transition of their wealth becomes, at best, a will, written with their lawyers and locked away to await their passing.

It would be so much better if the beneficiaries were prepared for the passing of the surplus wealth, the thinking was shared and explained, and better still if the beneficiaries were involved in the development of the purpose, goals and objectives.

4. Managing surplus wealth

I have considered in this section the purpose of wealth and the people it will affect. The final stage to consider is the process by which the issues surrounding surplus wealth will be managed. Process is important as it will be the means by which you try to ensure the surplus wealth is sustained for the future purpose – and the people – identified.

Surplus wealth suffers natural entropy, so the absence of process to achieve the opposite will see it gradually decline and disappear. A number of different forces are at play:

- **Fragmentation:** Surplus wealth is unlikely to grow in line with the growth in the size of the family, and that's before throwing in divorce or other family disputes. Clear objectives and clear investment strategies will have to be put in place and clear decisions taken regarding beneficiary numbers and distributions if the wealth is to survive generations.
- **Trust and communication:** Research tells us that up to 60% of wealth transition failures are down to the failure of trust and communication.[7] My own experience and research in dealing with families is that levels of trust and communication are far lower than the family members think, most particularly in the senior gencration. And it's mostly unintentional.
- **Preparation:** Again, research tells us that lack of preparation of

the next generation is a major cause of wealth transition failure,[8] but I see the lack of preparation as more significant than that. So many of the issues I experience are to do with lack of preparation of and by the senior generation – preparation of themselves for what they face, as well as preparation of the beneficiaries.

- **Unclear decision making:** While the senior generation are alive, decision making tends to be vested in or led by them, or put off. Once they've gone, unless a structure has been put in place, quite simply anything can happen.

And so to the question of the management process, which I refer to as family governance. The focus of this book is an explanation of how an appropriate, well-structured family governance system can support a family in the successful management of their surplus wealth.

Part II:
The role of family governance in managing surplus wealth

1. Defining family governance

The focus of family governance throughout this book is on the systems and processes for managing surplus inter-generational family wealth.

This differs from the more traditional focus of family governance which tends to look at governance in family-owned businesses. The family business-focused version of family governance looks at corporate governance (covering the direction for business operations and strategy) and family governance (providing a framework of rules that define family members' roles and responsibilities, and how the family interact with their business).[9]

The way I look at family governance in this book broadens the focus from just governance relating to the family business to governance relating to surplus family wealth, where that wealth may or may not include a family business or business interests. The focus on governance of the family – and the interaction between the two – remains.

So while the approach shares many of the same characteristics, it enables us to cover a wider, and increasingly common, span of family wealth situations. Examples I have dealt with include significant financial investments, property, art and other collectibles, and even family philanthropy.

Crucial is the idea that all or some significant part of the wealth is to be maintained for family-wide, rather than individual, purposes and interests, and that the family has a shared wealth purpose to reflect this. If the intention is to just split up the wealth between the heirs there is much less, if any, need for family governance.

Family governance of inter-generational surplus family wealth, as I define it in this book, requires six elements:[10]

- a culture and structure of open family communication;
- the valuing of family overall above individual or family branch needs;

- a demonstrated competence in assigning responsibilities;
- an effective succession plan for the continuity of the family wealth;
- family conflict management processes; and
- the maintenance of an effective family governance plan.

The importance of these elements can't be overstated and they should be built into the family's governance framework. While Part III of this book will demonstrate how they can be so integrated, it's worth taking a look at them to understand why they are so important.

1.1 Open family communication

I have already highlighted how failure of trust and communication plays a significant role in wealth transition failure. Research I have undertaken with families shows not only the importance of open family communication, but also how easily families, particularly parents, make assumptions about the levels of communication and understanding between the generations.

I have found this communication gap to be true even in families who are actively engaged in working together on an inter-generational wealth transfer strategy. Failures share the following characteristics:

- Parents consistently rate the sense of having a shared family wealth purpose much more highly than the next generation.
- Parents believe the shared purpose to have been co-created with the next generation much more strongly than the next generation does.
- Parents rate themselves strongly as being good communicators and having communicated clearly; the next generation doesn't share the same feeling.

Much of what is going on here is borne out by the way in which the next generation perceive these discussions with their parents. The information in the table below comes from discussions I have had with groups of next-generation members of families with surplus wealth.

Table 1: Inter-generational perceptions and expression of worries

Next-generation perceptions of parental worries	Next-generation expression of their own worries
Tax	Fear and insecurity; a worry they will be seen as entitled
Next-generation loyalty to the senior generation	A sense of guilt and confusion
Trust	Concerns that their parents are worried about trust and honesty
Doubts about partners and children	Lack of clarity and knowledge about parents' intentions
Love and care	A sense of responsibility along with recognition that they have big shoes to fill
Fairness	Recognition of the need for personal growth
Future consequences	

There is a communication gap, and this highlights two problems. The first is the gap itself – that there can be such differences even where there appears an expressed interest in doing things together. The second is that where the existence of the gap is a function of poor communication, it means that there is no mechanism to close it or deal with other issues where open communication is required.

1.2 Valuing family overall

This is about more than a family having a shared purpose; it's about recognising that to achieve the shared purpose the family members or branches have to fully buy into that shared purpose and be prepared to back it over their own individual needs. This commitment needs to be for the long term – effectively permanent. It's not something that can be opted in and out of.

This will in all likelihood mean that individual and family branch needs are not met on an equal basis, as not all will play the same role. This in turn will require a strong emotional commitment to the family that is capable of counterbalancing or overcoming a purely rational or individual need assessment.

And as families grow and family branches develop, there will be a need for incoming family members to buy into that ethos, even though they haven't developed as part of it, and then to impart it to the next generation. It might require them to subvert their own family approaches to the new family shared purpose. Quite an ask!

1.3 Competence in assigning responsibilities

If individual or family branch need is going to be subjugated to overall family needs, the system put in place to manage the family needs will have to be administered on a competent basis, by members of the family capable of doing so and trusted to do so by other members of the family, who are in turn accepting of the outcome.

This requirement throws up many interesting issues:

- how to judge the level of competence required;
- what benchmarks are set or used;
- the transparency of the requirements for roles;
- fair selection processes;
- the basis for reaching and making decisions;
- the way in which decisions can or cannot be appealed; and
- the way the system renews and regenerates itself.

And that's not all. Within the family governance architecture, one of the critical areas of decision making is the appointment of individuals to key roles, whether family or non-family members, to positions regarding the family business or surplus wealth, or within the governance mechanisms relating to the family.

With access to power and influence second only to access to money as a source of family conflict, this is an area ripe for problems and difficulties.

Much family conflict will either flow from or be avoided by the level of competence demonstrated in these areas.

1.4 An effective succession plan

One of the areas in family governance where I often see less focus than there should be is in the area of succession planning for the continuity of the family wealth.

For family businesses, family wealth and family governance, succession should be about the long game. And it doesn't just relate to family members, it relates to non-family members in the business (such as senior managers and non-executive directors) and non-family members involved in the management of the family wealth (such as trustees or investment professionals), as well as professional advisers (such as lawyers, accountants and bankers).

Nor does it only relate to the skills and competences to do a job – it relates to the development of an emotional attachment to, and ownership of, the values, ethos and vision associated with the family's wealth.

Development of the next generation of family wealth leaders takes many years, and it starts during their early and teen years, not just when they start to think about careers. For example, if a family member wants to build the expertise to run the family investment office, they should aspire to be as good as the best external hires, and that is not something that can be learnt on the job. The net should be spread wide within the family, so that opportunities are not just seen as being available to the sons and daughters of the current leaders – the next best CEO of the family business might be the niece or nephew of a family member not in the business.

As for non-family members at the heart of the family wealth, typically not governed by terms set out in corporate governance codes, they can and do become trusted advisers. But what happens when they need to be replaced?

This important topic needs to be thought of as much more than just succession planning – it needs to be about long-term thinking and actions that will support the continuity of the family wealth for generations.

1.5 Family conflict management processes

A good system of family governance will be designed to minimise, mitigate or manage conflict within the family, but it won't and can't eliminate it. So a conflict management process will need to be designed. Conflict, here, is not the same as healthy debate which, once had, results in acceptance of the way forward.

Conflict management typically requires a set of rules to be in place that is accepted by all who are subject to them, and that provides clarity about how decisions are reached and taken across all aspects of the family wealth and governance framework.

It also requires mechanisms, vested in people within the governance framework, for their maintenance and for adjudication on any decisions required. There clearly needs to be transparency about how this all works so members of the family can see that any decisions taken are in line with the processes, but equally important is that the system is designed in a way that reinforces alignment and minimises the reward for divergence.

Notwithstanding the foregoing, it has to be recognised that more fundamental conflicts may emerge. What can't be predicted is precisely where and how such conflicts will rise to the surface. Consequently there needs to be a way that they can be dealt with, even if it means designing exit arrangements.

1.6 Maintenance of an effective family governance plan

An effective family governance plan is the thing that can bring all of the foregoing elements together. But it doesn't stand still – it needs to be capable of dealing with constantly moving parts relating to the family's surplus wealth, and within the family, and to recognise the forces of growth (whether with regard to the surplus wealth or the family) and the headwinds or forces of entropy that will be faced.

So a maintenance plan is required. A plan that deals with all of these challenges, whether they be the little niggles, the unexpected emergencies or the long-term anticipated changes.

The six elements of family governance explored above provide a strong sense of what family governance of surplus wealth requires, and provide a glimpse of why it's required and how it can help. In the next section we will take a deeper look at why families with surplus wealth really do need family governance.

2. Why do families with surplus wealth need family governance?

As the last section has shown, there are many reasons why families should set up a governance system, but I want to focus on three. The first, I believe, is particular to families with surplus wealth whereas the second and third might also be experienced by other families.

2.1 Complexity

Complexity can come from many sources including:

- the sheer range, size and scope of family business interests;
- complex family demographics covering multiple generations and international locations, and sometimes extended families from multiple relationships; and
- a complex web of wealth structures based on genuinely well-meaning professional advice, but often received in a piecemeal fashion as the family's wealth develops rather than with full consideration of the family's circumstances and goals or a sense of how those structures need to operate to achieve a harmonious outcome.

2.2 Family conflict

We know that money and power are two of the key sources of family conflict, and very wealthy families, almost by definition, have both. Add in the risk of unrealistic and unfulfilled expectations, real or perceived, and you're probably just a step or two away from an outbreak of family conflict.

2.3 Communication issues

Research tells us that poor levels of trust and communication are at the root of as many as 60% of inter-generational wealth failures.[11]

So what happens with families who, far from having a well-organised family governance system, have deeply complex, poorly understood set-ups and may lack the communication and trust necessary to work through issues of conflict?

As nature abhors a vacuum, so families will establish some method of organising themselves – what we might refer to as natural governance, a model for which is demonstrated in Figure 1.

In my experience, natural governance tends to have some or all of the following characteristics:

- a central driving or controlling force for direction and decision making, usually the patriarch or matriarch;
- bilateral relationships between other family members that primarily flow from the patriarch or matriarch;
- a lack of family-wide discussions and a lack of open information and sharing that starts off as a way of trying to reduce conflict and argument, but can end up causing increased levels of distrust;
- coping mechanisms aimed at the avoidance, rather than management, of family conflict; and
- bilateral relationships with external advisers that reinforce the siloed approach to power and information.

Saying this doesn't mean that natural governance is always bad. Many families cope perfectly well with this sort of model. But equally, and

Figure 1. Natural governance model

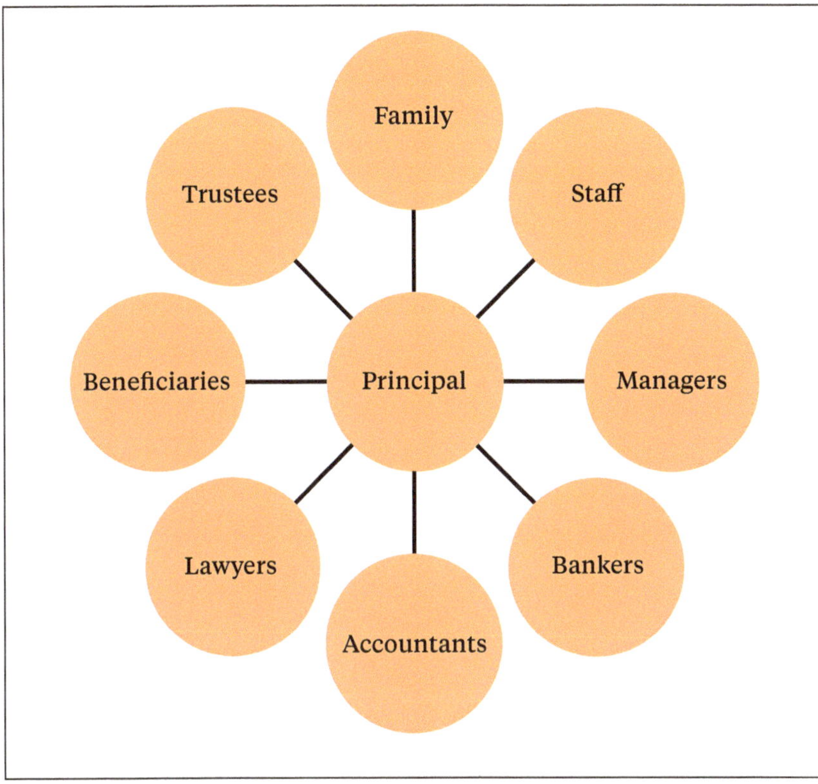

Source: Author.

without being overly dramatic, models of natural governance based on the diagram above can also share a number of characteristics, albeit in a mild way, with dysfunctional families:[12]

- lack of empathy and respect towards family members;
- conflict and hostility;
- secrecy, denial and rigid rules;
- emotional behaviour and blaming family members;
- using children as weapons; and
- conditional support.

Each family is of course unique, with its own set of behaviours and characteristics – some helpful, others less so. And all this happens inside discrete family units that have limited mechanisms for comparative learning and development, so it's really hard to get a view on what works well for all families.

Some families do manage to find a state of natural governance that could be described as 'balanced' or 'in equilibrium' that enables them to manage, and there are of course families who have succeeded in managing surplus wealth through the generations based on a model of natural governance.

My view, though, is that even when working well, many – far more than might be expected – natural governance set-ups exist in what I describe as a state of 'stable dysfunctionality'. The question is how much dysfunctionality there is and what coping mechanisms are in place within particular families to sustain that stability.

I am reminded of the opening line of Tolstoy's *Anna Karenina*:

> *Happy families are all alike; every unhappy family is unhappy in its own way.*

To understand this more it can be helpful to look further at the characteristics of dysfunctional families, where we see labels such as 'conflict families', 'chaotic families', 'dominant families' or even 'emotionally distant families' being used.

And as we look into some of the causes listed we see things such as:

- authoritarian parents;
- soft parents;
- absent parents;
- large, extended families;
- unfortunate life events;
- systematic instability; or
- a history of dysfunctionality.

I think it's fair to say that most parents in wealthy families don't set out with the aim of attracting one of the labels in the list above. But many parents may well end up displaying or experiencing some of these tendencies, even to a mild degree, often as a consequence of what it took to create their success in the first place or the drivers of much of the family conflict seen in wealthy families – money and power. And they lack the communication mechanisms to deal with the fallout.

On top of this, family histories, unplanned life events, circumstances, relationship dynamics and career choices can all be factors that lie behind the parental behaviours listed above. And in the same way that these issues might have been experienced by the parents in their formative years, they can play out in the next generation.

On the other hand, if we look at the characteristics of healthy families, we see the following:[13]

- individual character, interests and emotional expression allowed and accepted;
- obvious and consistent rules and boundaries;
- consistent, respectful treatment of family members, with flexibility to meet individuals' needs;
- feelings of safety and security;
- care for children provided by parents;
- age-appropriate responsibilities given; and
- perfection acknowledged to be unattainable and unrealistic.

Very different to the previous list, but to me these sound like the very principles, values or elements that one would like to see in well designed and balanced family governance systems.

3. Family governance and transition

Life, of course, doesn't stand still. So even if a family reaches a happy state of balance, equilibrium or even stable dysfunctionality, events will happen. The system needs to be able to adapt and change. The baton will have to be passed on. And these moments of transition can see the system improve or deteriorate. It won't stay the same – it can't. And the surplus wealth still has to be dealt with.

In introducing the concept of the natural entropy of wealth we have already highlighted a number of potentially harmful forces at play. These can be exacerbated by discrete events – births, deaths, marriages, divorce, ill-health. They could be prompted by the natural growing and ageing process, where the meaning and purpose of life for family members changes; or by a failure to recognise and deal with the emotions of life-changing events.

While families regenerate, where surplus wealth is concerned there is a specific generation that will be responsible for its creation. For our purposes it becomes the first generation.

The first generation have children. Brothers and sisters, should they have children, bring cousins into the family dynamic. The number of children in each generation can radically affect the spread of the family tree. Spouses and partners can reinforce the emergence of family branches, as in-laws bring in the influences, practices and behaviours of other families, and don't have the shared experiences and upbringing of the bloodline.

The generations and family branches won't grow evenly in number or time. They'll spread internationally. And as this happens there will be less shared time together, with fewer common interests.

And as they develop, the generations will see the future and the world differently. Think of how the baby boomers, Gen X, millennials and Gen Z differ. World history and events shape lives and attitudes. Family change is overlaid with societal change.

All of which means that families not only need to deal with events, they need to counteract the natural and unseen forces we've outlined – forces, let's be honest, most don't even recognise, let alone deal with – in a planned and organised way. They need to keep evolving to manage generational transition, just as they will need to evolve their management of the surplus wealth.

Elements that, in my experience, will help to make this more successful include:

- a clear sense of purpose;
- convening the generations;
- harnessing difference;
- communication;
- building trust; and
- preparing the next generation.

In other words, the emergence of a system. A system that – unlike most cases of natural governance – evolves with shared purpose, strategy and the involvement of those it affects.

But again we can find the forces of nature are against us. Families, largely being closed units, are unlikely to suddenly have a eureka moment, and just start evolving a new strategic system of family governance. More likely, some external event will trigger consideration of the need to get organised. While pressure for change in a family can come from many sources, action has to be supported from the top. Only when the top is ready will change happen.

And so we encounter another potentially adverse force of nature – increasing life expectancy. With the senior generation likely to be around for longer – fitter and healthier, too – there's a risk that they're less willing to pass on the baton. And underneath them we will see a stacking up of the generations, with all the potential for complexity, lack of communication and conflict and rivalry that entails.

To quote Gladys Hunt, "Parents must decide what quality of family life they will have and then use the necessary discipline to accomplish this. Otherwise life will push the family in diverse directions."[14]

4. When and how family governance develops

As natural governance feels, well, natural, and given that families have little practical knowledge or understanding of how other families organise themselves, in my experience it takes a specific event or series of events for a family to consider the need to think about the way they organise themselves. Typically these events need to be of sufficient importance or impact for the effect to be felt – and the effect needs to be felt by a senior member of the family.

The table below provides a number of catalytic events that I have seen cause a family to start the process of considering how they are organised.

Table 2. Catalysts for family governance arrangements

Family business issues	• A family member joins or leaves employment in the business. • There is a discussion about the level of pay for a family member who works in the business. • A non-family member is appointed to a senior business position, or a non-family member acquires shares in the family business. • Key business personnel – family or non-family – retire. • There is an opportunity for business expansion or a threat of contraction. • An offer is made for the company or the company decides to explore external investment or ownership.
Family issues	• Key life-stage transitions are reached; mainly when each generation wants and needs to know what will happen in future (seniors 65–80 and next generation 35–50). • Unexpected illness or accident affects a family member or someone very close to the family. • There is a marriage, a divorce or the arrival of children or grandchildren. • Hostilities break out somewhere in the business that threaten family harmony – or in the family that threaten the business.

Family wealth issues	• A share-owning trust is created, or a trust settled. • Someone inherits shares. • There is a build-up in pressure for more dividends or the opportunity to sell shares. • There is an impetus to build family philanthropy.
Reputational issues	• The family's or owners' privacy is breached; there is unwelcome media coverage of family/owners. • A breach of confidentiality occurs; someone uses private information for their own profit. • There is dishonesty, or misuse of company credit for personal gain.
Other	• Changes take place in the external environment that are perceived as, alternatively, threatening or an opportunity – general election, recession, legal and tax changes.

Even the occurrence of a clear catalytic event doesn't mean that families will start to get organised. Making a shift from thinking about doing something to actually doing it – moving from natural to organised governance – means changing what are often deeply embedded behaviours, relationships or even family power structures. And change doesn't happen easily.

For change to happen, the benefits of making the change have to outweigh the costs as well as any loss of the benefits of the status quo. Moving from the status quo means letting go of certain things and trading certainty for uncertainty – something people find pretty difficult to do. The more so, those people holding the strings of power.

Likewise in the context of families. Families are understandably reluctant to tinker with the carefully balanced stable dysfunctionality;

they know from personal experience what can happen in families when that stability is disturbed.

That said, there is perhaps one overriding piece of advice about this. Making the change when times are good and before it is needed is so much easier than trying to do so in difficult or stressful times. Yet experience shows that all too often families delay and defer, using the fact that things are okay today as the reason to put things off until tomorrow.

Before the development of a system of family governance can happen, we need to undertake an assessment of where the family is today. Family governance is not developed and implemented from a textbook or by adopting best practices; it develops incrementally from wherever the family and/or the family business is today – its starting point.

4.1 Assessing a family's natural governance

A starting point for assessing a family's natural governance is to see how the characteristics of the family compare with those of the healthy and/or dysfunctional families that we explored in section 2 above, "Why do families with surplus wealth need family governance?", and which are summarised in Table 3.

While the aim is to see which of the various characteristics are judged to apply to the family, the process absolutely shouldn't be bluntly applied. Do not just send out a list and ask for scores out of 10; rather, conversations should be held with family members and the topics explored and assessed in that way. This assessment should be carried out with a broad range of, if not all, family members, as different members of the family will have different perceptions and perspectives that will enable a picture to be created around the existence of these characteristics.

Another way of approaching this is to encourage family members to have a series of one-on-one conversations with other members of the family to explore the following:

- the things the other family member does that really support and develop strong family relationships;

Table 3. Family characteristics: healthy vs dysfunctional

Healthy[15]	Dysfunctional[16]
Individual character, interests and emotional expression allowed and accepted	Lack of empathy and respect towards family members
Obvious and consistent rules and boundaries	Conflict and hostility
Consistent, respectful treatment of family members, with flexibility to meet individuals' needs	Secrecy, denial and rigid rules
Feelings of safety and security	Emotional behaviours and blaming family members
Care for children provided by parents	Using children as weapons
Age-appropriate responsibilities given	Conditional support
Perfection treated as unattainable and unrealistic	

Source: Author – the table is based on the lists in Basem A Al-Ubaidi's 2017 article (see fn 12).

- the key blockers that prevent the family really working well together;
- which of the many positive things could they do even more of; and
- how the family might tackle some of the blocking issues.

The responses should be captured and the resulting material discussed with the family. The aim is to discuss the issues arising, not who said what about whom.

The next step is to see from where, why and how these characteristics appear in the family culture. One approach for doing this is to use an adapted form of the 'cultural web' shown in Figure 2 below.[17] Originally developed for use in identifying culture within a company, it can be used just as well for either the family business or the family itself. The natural governance and culture of a family will be driven by the results of the assessment of each of the six elements in the cultural web and by the way in which they interact. What we are looking to do here is to try to understand which of the various elements drive the particular characteristics of the family's culture and governance – and, of course, who in the family plays what role in relation to these things.

When it comes to assessing for the existence of the characteristics in Table 3, I see them as falling into two groups. The first group covers the three circles in the top half of Figure 2 – they are more to do with the way the family builds its narrative. The second group covers the three circles in the bottom half, which are about how the family organises itself.

As noted earlier, in carrying out such an exercise it is important to get as many members of the family involved as possible (subject to a minimum age threshold). For this part, family members should do the exercise independently, not in pairs or groups. Depending on the size of the family, the information can then be aggregated to present a picture back to the family of its culture. Looking at the information by generation or by family branch might add some additional insight and value.

While we should now have an established baseline understanding of the natural governance of the family, there are three preconditions for the development of a family governance system for surplus wealth that we need to test for. (Before doing so, it's worth reminding ourselves that we are looking at situations where families have significant surplus wealth and where there is a greater likelihood that those families will want to sustain their wealth into future generations.)

Figure 2. The cultural web

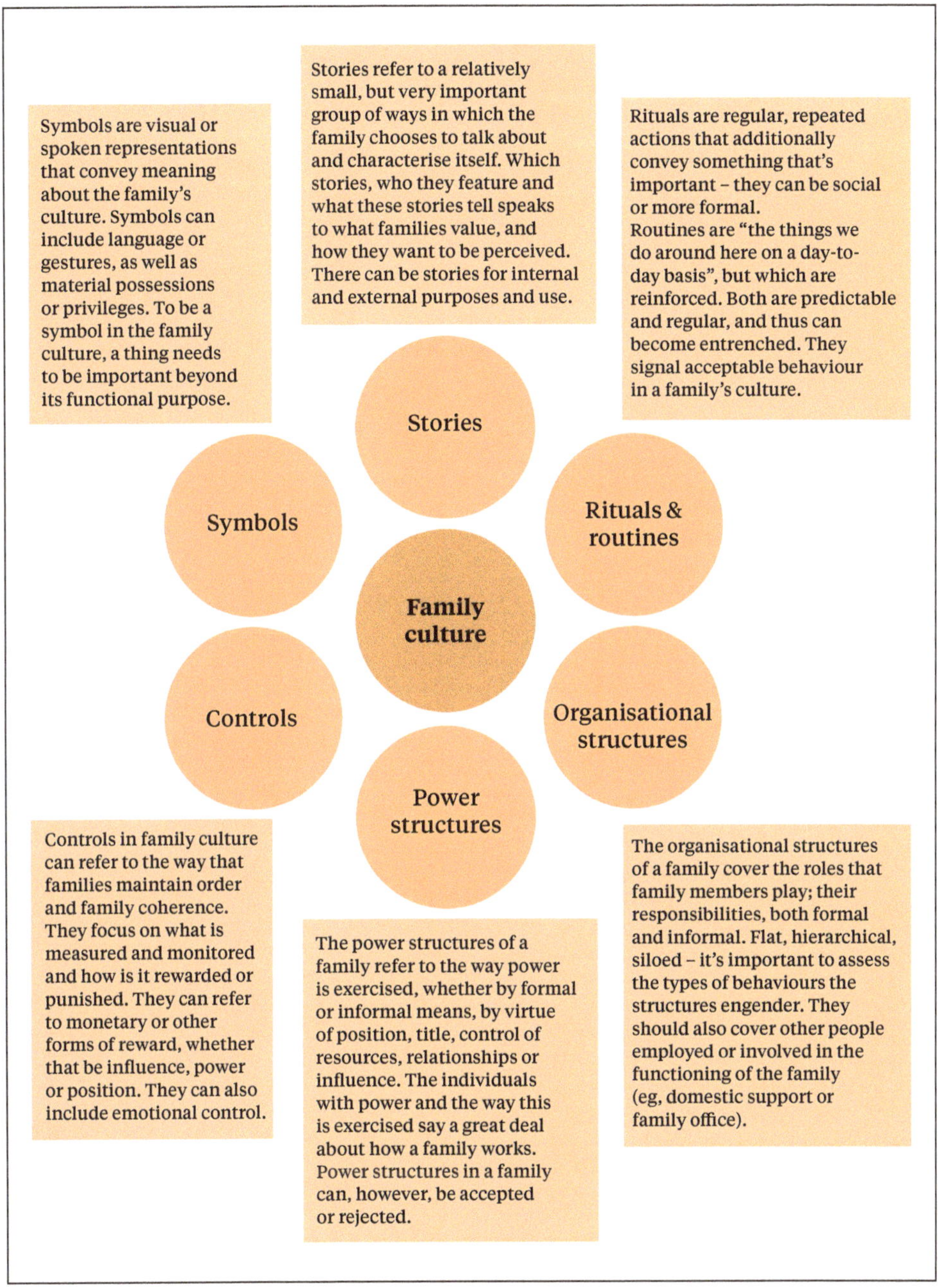

Source: Adapted from Gerry Johnson et al, Exploring Corporate Strategy *(see fn 17).*

"My experience has shown that it's one thing for families to work on defining a shared purpose, but quite another for the senior generation to recognise a need, and therefore show willingness, to get organised."

a. Desire for shared purpose
Family governance systems are most likely to thrive when there is a commonly agreed or shared purpose within the family for its surplus wealth. That's not the same as saying everyone will be able to benefit, whether equally or at all, from the surplus wealth, just that everyone agrees to and is willing to support the defined purpose or purposes of the wealth. Even better when the wider family has been involved in defining the shared purpose.

Yet we see many families where the plan for the family's surplus wealth is driven by the views of the senior generation. With the strategy firmly under the control of the senior generation, wider family have no role in establishing the purpose and may well have no role in the management of the surplus wealth. As mentioned, this approach can sometimes extend to attempts to control the wealth from the grave, with conditions and protections established to prevent the wider family from being able to participate in the subsequent control and management of the surplus wealth.

Maybe slightly more benign, but no less antithetical to family governance, some senior generations within families maintain close secrecy regarding the levels of surplus wealth, even from the family. There is no shared purpose in such families regarding their surplus wealth.

Family governance is unlikely to find a role or place in either of these situations.

b. Recognition of the need to get organised
My experience has shown that it's one thing for families to work on defining a shared purpose, but quite another for the senior generation to recognise a need, and therefore show willingness, to get organised.

This is about being prepared and willing to make the necessary change. Ordinarily the stronger the benefit of making the change, or the greater the cost of not making the change, the greater the likelihood that a family will get organised. Yet for many families, change doesn't happen because the cost of making the change, particularly for the senior generation (what we might call letting go) is just too high.

For change to take place, and often for a commitment to be given for change to take place, there needs to be a process for delivering change in which there is confidence.

c. Strong foundational values

As they say, where there's a will, there's a way. If the two factors above are about defining the will, strong foundational values within a family are a big part of defining the way. Strong, proven, tested family values are likely to be the foundation for the trust and communication required to enable a family to get itself organised.

This is a really important piece of the family governance jigsaw which we will look at more closely in Part III.

4.2 Development of family governance

I mentioned earlier that family governance builds from a given state of natural governance, or starting position, and that it requires a catalytic event to kick-start it. In this section I will look at six examples that show from where and how a more systematic approach to governance can develop.

The development of a governance system can start either with the family or with the family's surplus wealth, and in any of the following events or circumstances:

- a multiplicity of wealth structures;
- the separation of business ownership and management;
- the sudden arrival of surplus wealth;
- 'Plan A, Plan B';
- next-generation involvement in the family business or wealth management; or
- non-family members owning shares in the business.

a. A multiplicity of wealth structures

A common starting point for family governance is when a business owner sells their business and starts to look at how they are going to structure the surplus wealth that they generate from the sale.

In such circumstances, it's not uncommon for quite a number of structures to be set up for the management of that wealth. These might include trusts, private trust companies, corporate vehicles, family investment companies or charitable trusts and foundations. Each of the structures needs to be thought of in terms of governance, and of course the more of them that are established, the greater the need for coordination.

There are a number of potential questions to address:

- Is the overall purpose for the family's wealth clearly articulated?
- Is the purpose understood by the entire family, and to what extent were the family involved in its creation?
- Is it clear what role each of the structures plays in the overall purpose of the wealth, and do they work together?
- Is it clear what roles family members will play in relation to the surplus wealth and the structures and are they ready, capable and willing to play these roles?
- Are the structures coordinated with the family's estate and succession plans?
- Are the wider family clear about all of the details contained in the running and management of these structures?
- Are the relationships with the professional advisers supporting these structures set up properly, so as to involve the relevant members of the wider family? Or are they just managed bilaterally?
- Are the appropriate communication and decision-making channels in place?

Experience shows that many families in this situation don't think about, let alone take the opportunity to start progressing and organising, a governance framework. The reasons for this can be similar to those set out in the section on the arrival of surplus wealth, although typically families in this situation are more experienced than those considered in that example. Reasons for not taking action can include any of the following:

- Selling a business brings major personal and professional changes to the former business owner. Being caught up in the moment can prevent the necessary reflection.
- Advice is taken from or reliance is placed on family, friends or long-time advisers who don't provide the right level of experience or reference points; or no advice is taken at all.
- Family disharmony or disagreement, secrecy or fear prevent proper consideration of what needs to be done.
- Reliance is placed on the family's previous or existing ways of dealing with or managing money, including reliance on many of the individuals and advisers used.
- Finally, but not overly surprisingly, there is little or no understanding of the dynamics of surplus wealth.

For those families wanting to take action, the family governance response should include some or all of the following:

- establishing a clear purpose for the wealth in its new form;
- creating a clear articulation of the purpose of the wealth – a wealth philosophy – that encompasses both the financial and non-financial wealth (including family values) of the family;
- ensuring that the foregoing is reflected in estate plans;
- understanding who the beneficiaries of the wealth will be and how the wealth might affect their lives and the lives of those around them;
- ensuring that those operating or advising on the operation of the wealth structures understand and are aligned with the purpose of the wealth, the family values and the beneficiaries;
- establishing governance and management mechanisms for the structures, including proactive relationship development and management of the structures and advisers by well prepared and trained members of the family; and
- setting out succession plans for the external advisers and family members.

b. The separation of business ownership and management

This scenario looks at cases where the shareholders of a business and the senior management are separated. I have experienced two common situations where this can happen. In the first, the family owners recognise the need to strengthen the management team, perhaps in preparation for eventual exit from the business, and appoint a non-family, external CEO to the company.

In the second, typically seen in larger businesses, the business is owned by a group of family shareholders but they have appointed non-family members to run it. Let's assume that none of the family shareholders sit on the board, and that the family have appointed non-executive directors to represent them. In this scenario, we see a more acute range of challenges arising for the governance of the business:

- An insufficient level of business expertise and interest within the family shareholder group runs the risk that they will come to see their ownership of the shares as simply generating a financial return; this can chip away at their sense of being long-term, responsible family owners.
- Over time, there is a risk that as the shares are distributed to an ever-widening group of family members, they will have a more and more distant relationship with the business, the board and the management team.
- The family shareholders will still be required to take decisions that fall within their remit as owners, yet as the link between the shareholders in the business and the board and management team they have appointed to run the business on their behalf becomes more distant, the balance in the exercise of these powers can change significantly.
- The multiple layers – ownership, board and management – can give rise to misaligned interests or, worse still, conflicts of interest.
- Although succession planning should take place for all of the roles and structures within the business, individuals often end up in roles for very long periods of years.

For many business-owning families finding themselves in this situation, the problems can creep up on them over time, rather than the family grasping the opportunity to proactively progress the development of a clear governance framework from an early stage. The reasons for this vary, but will typically be along the following lines:

- Excessive stability, long service or the informal exercise of control by certain senior family members can shield the wider family from the need to prepare for succession.
- Reliance on trusted relationships can be preferred to exposing the company to mechanisms contained within corporate governance codes, which require the exercise of more transparent accountability.

For those families who do take action, governance arrangements might include some or all of the following:

- creating a forum, which we might refer to as a shareholder assembly, that has the aim of promoting responsible ownership within the family shareholder group and promotes clear understanding and communication between the shareholders and the board;
- clear board roles and responsibilities, including for the chair and perhaps even for a senior non-executive director;
- clear accountabilities and decision-making powers for senior management, the board and shareholders;
- robust and timely succession planning for key senior management positions, non-executive directors and the chair, with clear term limits set out;
- a strong alignment of return and reward between the various stakeholders;
- a clear understanding of the risks; or
- identification and management of potential conflicts of interest, with clear checks and balances.

c. The sudden arrival of surplus wealth

The arrival of surplus wealth is a good catalytic event to assess. It's a helpful scenario as it typically moves an individual or family from a position where the lack of surplus wealth means they will have had no reason to focus on family governance, to a situation where suddenly having an organised and systematic approach to the governance of their family and, now, surplus wealth would be extremely helpful to them.

While the particular scenario I have used below is that of a lottery winner, I have regularly encountered this sort of situation, particularly where business owners are exiting their business, in whole or in part, and in doing so generate a life-changing amount of liquid (as opposed to inaccessible) surplus wealth. I have also encountered it when a parent or grandparent makes or leaves a gift of significant wealth to a young person.

I've chosen to use the example of a lottery winner because I want to focus on the life-changing aspects that the sudden arrival of wealth often brings. It changes many lives. It throws up in the air assumptions about life, relationships and money. It can disrupt what were perfectly happy, if more ordinary, life trajectories. It exposes people to situations and decisions of which they have little knowledge or experience, and in all likelihood they will have to rely on the advice of strangers to help them.

One of the reactions I often hear from people who find themselves in this situation is that they want to keep many aspects of their life the same, but somehow enjoy the benefits of the newly found wealth. As the next section shows, this is rarely possible. And for those who do manage to hide their wealth from others, this is only temporary and has many unintended consequences of its own.

This scenario, then, sets up a number of potential issues that would need to be tackled:

- how to define and find new purpose (financial, personal and family) while staying in touch with the old and familiar;
- how to enjoy the new-found wealth but in a manageable, controlled way;
- how to prepare close family to deal with the change;
- how to manage relationships with wider family and friends;
- what strategies to put in place to manage and protect the wealth, whether that be relationships with advisers or setting up structures; and
- how to deal with the signalling that takes place, intentional or otherwise, and ensure a clear communication approach underpinned by values.

Experience shows that most families in this situation won't think about, let alone take the opportunity to start progressing and organising, a governance framework. The reasons for this vary but include the following:

- There is no family history, personal experience or other reference points for taking such action – this is the first generation in the family with surplus wealth.
- Being caught up in the moment – either in terms of enjoyment or panic – doesn't allow the necessary reflection.
- Advice is taken from, or reliance placed upon, family and friends who have no experience or reference points – or no advice is taken at all.
- Reliance is placed on the family's previous or existing ways of dealing with or managing money, and there is little or no understanding of the dynamics of surplus wealth.
- The family work with advisers who are happy to provide their specific services in return for a fee, but don't understand or think more broadly about the impact and implications of the newly found wealth. Governance is highly unlikely to feature in their thinking.
- The family may be at a life stage where they just can't think about long-term consequences.

On the other hand, some families will take matters in hand and do some or all of the following:

- take stock of their situation and access appropriate professional advice;
- think hard about what this newly acquired wealth (both core and surplus) means to them – what opportunities, but also what harm, it might bring; and ask themselves whether they want to continue, as best they can, their previous approach to life or let the wealth change their lives;
- explore the consequences of whatever approach is taken – both the intended or likely consequences, but more importantly the unintended and therefore unknown ones;
- think about the future roles of family members (for the first generation this could be to continue in employment, change job

or career, take up new activities or retire) and the impact on the next generation;
- work on establishing purpose for the newly found wealth and begin to set objectives for part or all of it;
- reflect on the family values that have sustained the family to date – whether the new wealth is likely to change those values, or whether those values might support the family in dealing with the new wealth;
- think about the impact the wealth and changed circumstances are going to have on the people the family know (this can be approached by thinking about concentric circles, starting with those closest and moving outwards towards friends, acquaintances and work colleagues); and
- put in place the necessary financial planning and protection measures for family and family members including, *inter alia*, wills, lasting powers of attorney, life assurance, estate planning and estate distribution plans, and asset protection structures.

The outcome can be the creation of a wealth narrative for the family – a golden thread that enables them to maintain cohesiveness when there is a real risk that the pressures of their wealth will act to drive them apart.

d. 'Plan A, Plan B'

I use the Plan A, Plan B approach for those with significant wealth or business owners who rationally understand the need to get organised, but emotionally would rather not confront the consequences of doing the detailed thinking, planning and organising that comes with having to plan for the future and to confront one's own mortality.

Plan A, Plan B recognises this by allowing for two scenarios:
- Plan A is where the individual survives for many more years and can therefore realise their long-term dreams in whatever way they wish.
- Plan B prepares for a scenario where the individual is not with us, and the very real risk that the wealth they have created is vulnerable to their premature departure.

"[A] will might document what happens to the wealth and/or ownership of the business, but that's not the same as having a plan for the continuity of the wealth or survival of the business when faced with the death of the owner/manager or driver of value for the wealth."

The governance planning starts with putting in place the minimum arrangements for a Plan B scenario, and then builds out from there as the individual's views and circumstances allow. In many cases, once the value of the Plan B approach is realised, the individual moves on to consider the governance needed to support Plan A.

This is not as difficult as it sounds, as often the individual will have prepared a will, a review of which becomes the starting point for the Plan B scenario – the will represents the default should something happen before any other planning is considered and put in place.

It can be helpful if, as is typically the case, the will was written many years ago, often well before the business became as successful or valuable as it is today. It usually needs to be updated, either because things have moved on since it was drafted or because the consequences of what the will contains have not been thought through in practical terms. The will might document what happens to the wealth and/or ownership of the business, but that's not the same as having a plan for the continuity of the wealth or survival of the business when faced with the death of the owner/manager or driver of value for the wealth.

This, then, sets up a number of potential family and family business questions that will need to be addressed:

- What degree of reliance is there, for the direction of the wealth or the success of the family business, on the wealth or business owner/manager?
- In the case of a family business, what are the management succession plans in the event that the owner/manager is no longer there?
- Again for a family business, what happens to the ownership of the shares – who becomes the new owner(s) of the family business? Do they understand the nature of the ownership role and how well prepared are they to take it on?
- Can these potential future management and ownership succession options viably work together?
- For family wealth, who will manage relationships with the professional advisers? Do they know who the advisers are? Is the

new owner of the wealth knowledgeable enough to manage the family's affairs?

- What financial and fiscal issues will arise on the passing of the owner/manager? How will the transition issues be financed? How will the long-term value of the family wealth or business be protected?
- What other critical third-party relationships within the family business would need to be managed?

Again, my experience shows that many wealthy families and family business owners don't recognise, let alone start to answer, these questions. Consequently, the opportunity to start or progress with organising a governance framework at an early stage is missed. The reasons for this vary, but are often one or other of the following:

- a focus on the day to day, or on the growth and development of the business;
- not wanting to focus on the consequences of one's own mortality, and the need to think them through in detail (I'm not sure whether this is because many of the questions just don't have answers or because business owners believe they'll live forever!);
- not wanting to share the scale of the wealth with the next generation; and
- not believing the next generation are ready.

For those families who do take action, the result in family governance terms will be likely to include some or all of the following:

- a process of deep reflection about the point and purpose of the family business or the family wealth and the personal and career aspirations of the owner/manager, perhaps examining the longer-term ownership transition options available;
- where family wealth is involved rather than a family business, mapping the management arrangements and the use of third parties, and looking at longer-term succession issues;
- for family business owners, examining the succession options for the business at both ownership and management levels with, as a first step, the development of management succession plans;

- reviewing the owner's willingness to plan more carefully the ownership succession arrangements, ensuring, *inter alia*, that they maximise value and minimise business interruption;
- ensuring there are appropriate arrangements in place to finance the transition without harming the value of the business or the family wealth;
- ensuring the governance and decision-making arrangements between the owners and managers in the business are coherent and up to date, and that in the event something happens to the owner, this documentation is readily available to the right people and is understood by them, so that appropriate actions are taken in a timely manner; and/or
- putting in place a communication framework that matches and supports the level of preparation.

Taking a Plan A, Plan B approach benefits the family by pulling together a coherent plan should something unexpected happen in the short term, while at the same time providing the family with a firm platform for the development of a longer-term solution.

e. Next-generation involvement

Another common starting point for family governance is where one or more members of the next generation want to join a family business. A variation on this scenario is where the senior generation of a family-owned business would like to gift some shares to the next generation.

This sets up a number of potential family and family business issues that will need to be tackled:

- transparency of treatment of the family members joining the business and those siblings or other family members not joining the business, in particular requirements about job experience and competencies, and decisions regarding future family members wanting to join;
- documenting the nature and scope of the employment in the business (remuneration and role profile);
- training and development, career development and performance management of the family member;

- perceptions of the family member by non-family employees and managers;
- if ownership of the business is shared, documentation of the terms, rights and responsibilities of owning the shares;
- ensuring that the legal documents behind the family and the family business are in order; and
- determining how communication and expectations between family members will be managed.

Again, experience shows that many family business owners don't take the opportunity to progress with organising a governance framework at this stage, for a number of reasons:

- There is a lack of strategic foresight for the family business.
- The next generation entering the business is seen as filling a tactical need rather than taking a strategic step in business succession, for the senior generation or the next.
- The senior generation don't want to cede control or even start to build a discussion about it.
- The family business is run on an informal basis, and arrangements within the family likewise, so it suits not to formalise things.
- The experience of the senior generation when they joined the business was of a similarly informal approach, and it makes sense to repeat their own experience with the next generation.
- The family may lack communication channels to approach arrangements on a more formal basis.
- The senior generation just don't see the need to build an organised approach to governance of the business or the family – there's a fear of *doing* something.

For those family businesses that do take action, however, the likely outcome in family governance terms might be some or all of the following:

- the setting of clear objectives for the continuation of the family business;
- recognition, clear definition and proactive management of the roles of key individuals, family and non-family;

- a focus on responsible ownership, eg, what this means in terms of commitments, exit provisions, reward and dividend strategy, and the governing documents of the organisation;
- the managing of family implications, eg, for family members not working in the business, the employment of in-laws, and the risk of divorce for a family member owning shares;
- a clear decision-making framework for the business and family;
- the creation of a family and family business communication framework; and
- the clarifying and establishing of shared family values.

Depending on precisely what level of involvement is being discussed for the next generation, a number of governance solutions might be implemented.

f. Non-family members owning shares in a family business

As a business grows, an entrepreneur or business owner may seek to incentivise the senior management team, or provide key members of the management team with a formal stake, and this may involve broadening the ownership base of the business.

A common alternative with the same characteristics is where a business may be owned by two or more individuals or business partners, not from the same family unit.

While from a business objective perspective these owners may share the same aims, given that the business is owned by individuals from different family units, it's almost certain they will not share the same personal or family financial objectives. Often age differences mean they have different personal aspirations beyond the business. These issues can be compounded where the size of the ownership stakes differ.

This difference between common business objectives and unshared personal objectives can give rise to a range of challenges:

- Differing personal financial objectives of the shareholders often affect the setting of the goals and objectives for the business, as

“Experience shows that when things are going well the absence of formal arrangements is rarely missed. In stressful or difficult times, however, the effect of their absence is magnified many times over.”

well as the development of the business strategy. This can affect growth strategies and can drive different attitudes to risk including a willingness or otherwise to fund the growth of the business.

- The responsibilities of the ownership and management roles can become blurred, which in turn can affect key decision making.
- Having both ownership and management stakes in the business can affect the way reward strategies are viewed and formulated.
- The question may arise as to what happens if one or more of the shareholders want to exit the business.
- With the death of a major shareholder, there is a very real risk that the controlling stake passes to people with no experience of the business, let alone running it or making major decisions.
- In time, frustration arises with the perception of uneven stakes in decision making and reward.

A significant number of business owners don't take the opportunity to proactively progress the development of a governance framework from an early stage. The reasons for this vary, but will typically be one or other of the following:

- A majority shareholder, one holding in excess of 50% of the shares, can effectively control decision making in the company through the ability to exercise the voting power of his or her equity stake. The availability of, or even threat of reliance on, this long-stop mechanism prevents the creation of a more formal framework for decision making.
- The company has successfully operated with a stable form of natural governance, meaning that there has been no drive to consider putting these issues on a more formal footing. To do so would mean having to tackle issues that the individuals find it easier to leave unspoken.

For those businesses that do take action, likely outcomes in governance terms might include some or all of the following:

- creating a formal shareholders' agreement that defines the relationship between the shareholders;
- establishing a clear decision-making framework for the company

at board and senior management levels, elements of which, if necessary, may be included in the articles of association or shareholders' agreement;

- ensuring that there's a clear remuneration strategy and framework that aligns reward with the interests of shareholders and management;
- making sure that there's a clear succession planning strategy at both shareholder and management levels;
- making key person protection and liquidity provision in the event of the death of a key director or shareholder; and
- ensuring that there are clear exit planning provisions in the event that a shareholder wants to sell his or her stake in the business.

Experience shows that when things are going well the absence of formal arrangements is rarely missed. In stressful or difficult times, however, the effect of their absence is magnified many times over.

This section has explored six examples of situations where family governance can start. They show that the governance developments are unlikely to just happen on their own. They require that inertia or a range of blockages or obstacles are overcome before they can be developed.

We can also see that the sorts of solutions that need to be developed are ones that, unless one has had previous experience of them, are unlikely to be internally generated.

Referring back to Figure 2, for a new governance system to emerge it's necessary for the content of all six elements of the cultural web to change. The scale of change required further highlights the level of the forces acting against that change.

The new governance outcomes or solutions that I've outlined will, most often, take place in the three elements in the lower half of the cultural web diagram. As they become embedded, the new governance arrangements should update many of the elements in the top half.

5. Summary

Part II has considered the need for and the role of family governance in relation to surplus wealth. I have explored examples of how family governance can start and demonstrated the forces that are acting to prevent the change happening and that need to be overcome.

We can see the challenges of moving from a scenario based on natural governance, where families have developed coping mechanisms to stay functional or prevent excessive levels of dysfunctionality, to a position with organised governance, requiring a strategic sense of purpose to design and create a system that allows the pursuit of an agreed common purpose, and that can proactively identify and deal with disagreement.

This challenge will be all the greater for families transitioning wealth between generations one and two, or two and three, where their model of governance is more likely a purely natural one, compared to families moving their wealth between generations four, five and six, where the next generations have grown up inside the parameters of a, by now, formulated system of natural or family governance that, as evidenced by its longevity, has proven successful.

It's worth reminding ourselves of the goals of family governance.[18] They highlight the importance of harnessing positive forces such as open communication, clarity, transparency and planning, but also illustrate some of the negative forces at play and how these have to be managed proactively:

- encouraging dialogue;
- planning and policy making;
- demarcating ownership and management;
- managing assumptions and expectations;
- adopting rules on potentially contentious issues; and
- managing conflict.

These goals cannot all be pursued at once. It's altogether too much to try to do so. They need to be tackled in a strategic and organised way. Consequently, when working with families on the development of a family governance framework, I work through three stages, which I have set out in Table 4.

Table 4. Family governance goals – purpose, people, process

Topic	Critical considerations
Purpose	• Identifying with the family the shared or common purpose for the family's wealth • Developing the family wealth narrative • Building an ethos of responsible ownership • Recognising the need for and making a commitment to change
People	• Identifying all of the stakeholders in the family wealth • Agreeing how they are going to be involved in the process • Creating an atmosphere of trust • Enabling constructive communication • Identifying the core and common family values • Determining how succession will be handled, for the senior and next generations • Balancing the roles and interests of family members
Process	• Creating the governance framework • Building the rules for decision making and communication • Developing the implementation steps • Ongoing family member training and development programmes • Managing the resulting governance framework

Part III:
Elements of family governance

1. Introduction

In Parts I and II we looked at what family governance is, and how and why it can develop. Part III takes a detailed and practical look at how a family governance framework is set up and operated. We will focus on what the different elements of the governance framework can be designed to do, how they can be operationally structured, and the issues and options to be considered for each element.

Part III works through:

- examples of governance structures, and the many elements that they might contain;
- how the family vision statement articulates the family's overall intention for its wealth; and
- how the elements of a governance structure can be designed and used, as well as the wide range of considerations that need to be taken into account for each element.

Importantly, the governance structures discussed below are assumed to arise through the processes set out in the earlier sections of this book, namely that the family works together to establish the purpose, people and processes for the governance of its surplus wealth. This approach means that the family have the opportunity to design the governance system with the aim of sustaining wealth through generational transition; the legal form and documentation follows the creation of the governance system that has been designed. It also means that each family will be intimately involved in the creation of its own future governance framework, built upon the foundations of its own unique natural governance.

This is particularly important when it comes to the trust-based example, as the approach differs from that seen in the creation of many trusts, where the settlor establishes the trust and sets out their own intentions for the wealth they are placing in trust. Often in these cases the trust has been established with a view to asset protection or the exertion of control. Consequently the trust documentation is designed from the settlor's (potentially protective or negative) point of view rather than being focused on an enabling governance structure for the benefit of future beneficiaries.

2. Governance structures

The ownership and governance structures set out below are purely for illustration purposes. They include a wide range of the possible supporting elements of a family governance architecture.

Figure 3 shows an example of a corporate-based family governance model, which is fairly typical where there is a significant family-owned business – albeit the family will typically own other assets – or where the family's wealth is held through one or more corporate structures. It is also regularly encountered in families with a large number of business interests or structures for their wealth. It's not unusual to encounter 10, 20 or even 30 corporate entities beneath the family holding company.

By its nature, a corporate-centred model means that the approach to governance will interact heavily with and use provisions available through company law. This means that such structures will vary according to the nature of the underlying company law of the jurisdictions in which the assets and companies are based.

In practice it is very unlikely that all of the governance elements shown in Figure 3 will be present in one governance structure, except perhaps in the case of the largest and most complex families or where the governance framework has been formed over an extended period.

In Figure 4 the assets of the family are held in trust. Central to this model is the role of the trustees, as legal owners of the family assets. The position and role of the trustees need to be taken into account in the way in which the trust deed and, if there is one, the letter of wishes of the settlor, are drawn. This becomes even more important once the settlor has passed away as it becomes fixed guidance to the trustees thereafter. Trustees, therefore, become hugely important stakeholders in the family's governance framework, and thought needs to be given to the way that relationship is managed.

Figure 3. Corporate-based family governance model

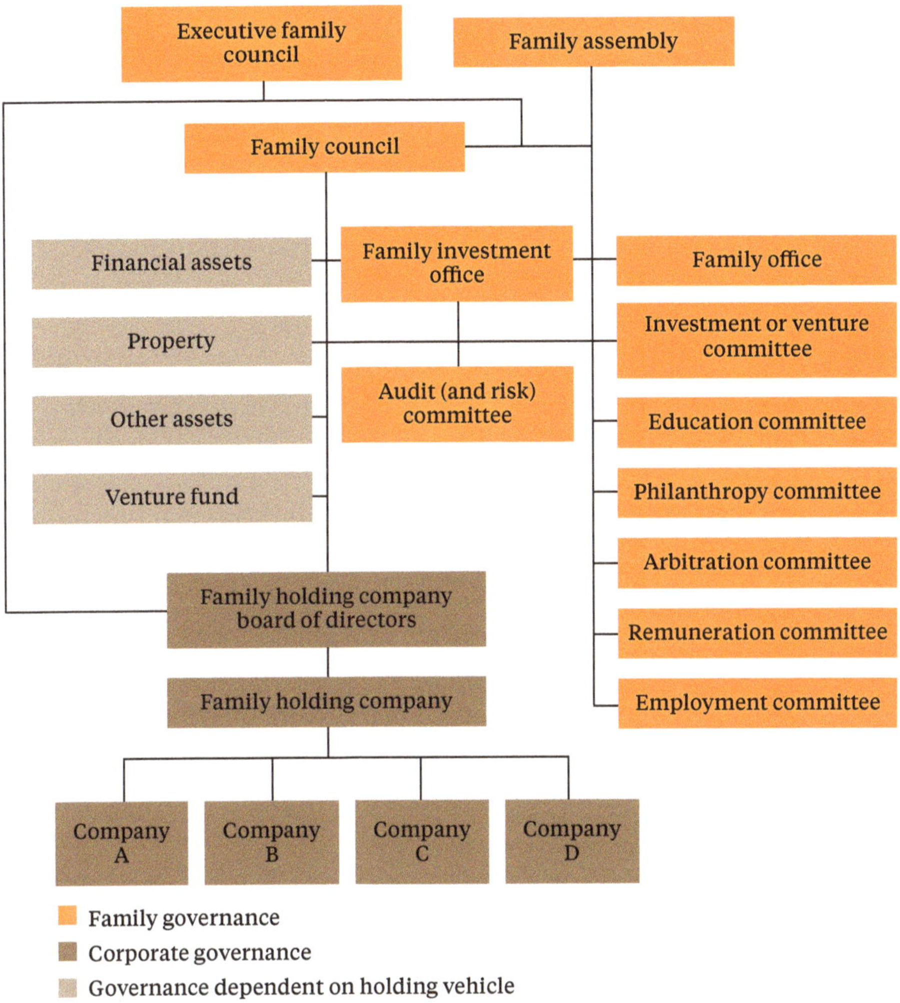

Source: Author.

Another key difference, in family governance terms, between a trust- and a corporate-based model is the existence of beneficiaries. Specifically, thought needs to be given to the education and development of beneficiaries as well as the development of the relationship between trustees and beneficiaries. While many of the family elements can be the same as in Figure 3, a number of the governance elements sitting under the family assembly and family council can be adapted for a trust-based structure – in Figure 4 it can be seen that they connect to the trust as well as to the family.

The roles played by the family governance elements in a trust-centred model, particularly those linked to the beneficiaries, become really important after the death of the settlor, as the legal owners – the trustees – are often not part of the family and the instructions and guidance in respect of the wealth held in the trust come from legal documents, rather than from the owner's own wishes.

While for both corporate- and trust-based structures there will come a point at which the current generation will not have had personal interaction with the founding generation, the introduction of a non-family element, in the form of non-family trustees, exacerbates this point of difference. Thought therefore needs to be given to how the effects can be mitigated.

Each element in a governance structure should play a specific role in the governance of the family's affairs and delivery of the family's wealth philosophy and objectives. Whether each element is required, the role it needs to play, and the individuals represented in that element are determined as the family governance framework is planned and developed.

For each element, a clear articulation of purpose, responsibility and accountability should be set out. It's important that the family members both involved in and affected by any element of the governance structure buy into what it is there to achieve. The aggregation of all of this detail is often summarised in the form of the family protocols, family charter or family constitution.

The family can choose the extent to which the governance arrangements are hard-wired into the legal documentation that underpins the family wealth, and the structures through which it is held, or left as matters agreed but not formalised legally. There are of course pros and cons to these two approaches.

Figure 4. Trust-based family governance model

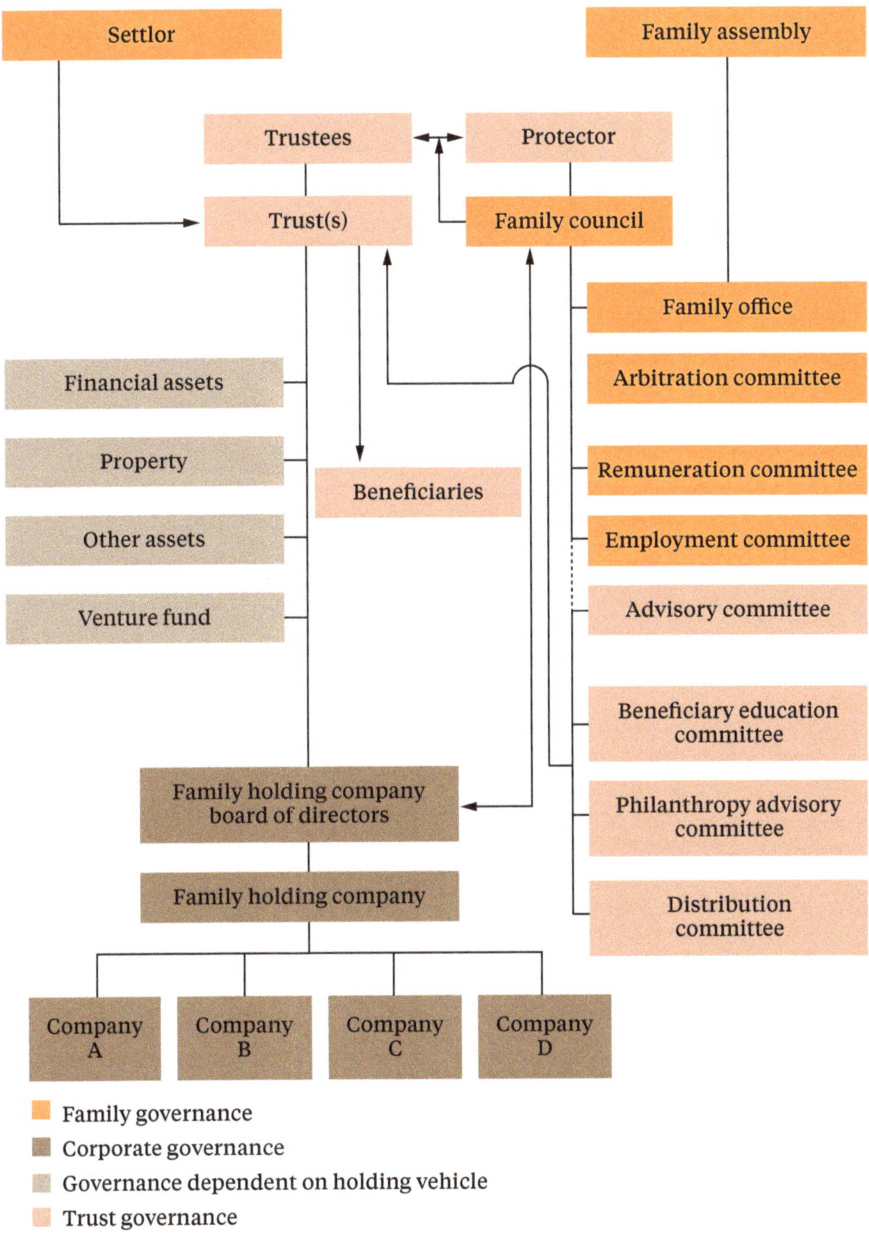

Source: Author.

A small number of elements are encountered frequently in family governance frameworks:

- family council;
- family assembly; and
- management board of the family company.

These tend to be the pivotal elements in the governance and management of a family's wealth and affairs. Particular attention should be paid to the way in which they are defined, established and used.

In the sections that follow we will take a detailed look at all of the governance elements shown in Figures 3 and 4.

3. Family vision statement

Key to the establishment of a family governance framework is the family vision statement, which sets out the point and purpose, goals and objectives for the family's surplus wealth – what I summarise as the family's wealth philosophy. The family governance framework is built to support the delivery of these goals and objectives, and avoid or mitigate risks to their sustainability.

Not only does the wealth philosophy provide clarity for the governance framework and the legal structures, but it also provides clarity for the people, both family and non-family, involved. And this philosophy has to be strong enough and sufficiently well articulated to provide clarity into the future.

Many families with significant wealth get trapped in a mindset aimed at protecting the wealth, and protecting members of the family from the afflictions it can cause. Such families tend to over-focus on the things that can go wrong, from family disagreements and conflict, to difficulties caused by in-laws, to divorce or even harmful habits and behaviours associated with so-called excess wealth, whether that be spending in general, gambling, drink or even drugs. Families with such views often worry about the way the surplus wealth may dim or diminish aspiration, drive and motivation in the next generation. Control and secrecy often become the behavioural drivers behind the approach to the family's wealth.

While these issues can't be overlooked, and taking appropriate steps to protect the family from harm and wealth fragmentation would seem entirely sensible, an alternative and, in my view, far better place to start these conversations is with thoughts about how the wealth can enhance, develop and support the lives of the members of the family, or be a force for good in society. And then to develop action plans aimed at achieving these more positively focused objectives, while recognising the risks. A thought comes to mind when I reflect on this: good behaviour begets good behaviour, negative behaviour begets negative behaviour.

So many of the difficulties encountered in the management and transition of family wealth stem from this point. Subsequent family disagreements and even family conflict can be traced back to a lack of clarity on the point and purpose of the wealth, and people's misunderstanding about what it means for them. It explains why a breakdown in trust and communication is the primary reason for failure of wealth transition.

A family vision statement would be likely to contain some or all of the following elements.

3.1 Wealth ownership and continuity philosophy

This should summarise the core philosophy of the family and its wealth, making reference to the timeframe, the overall goals, the form(s) of the wealth, and what it means for the different generations and branches as the family and the wealth evolve.

It is, of course, easier to articulate the positive aspects of the wealth philosophy, but it's equally if not more important to articulate what the wealth philosophy doesn't cover or isn't meant to provide.

"Purpose that is built on a process that involves the family in its creation brings a sense of commitment and ownership to the outcomes."

3.2 Purpose and objectives of the family's wealth

Surplus wealth without clear purpose and objectives is likely to cause or be seen as generating inconsistency and confusion, unequal or unfair favour or treatment, and very possibly harm and difficulty within a family. Different views and perspectives without a unifying, consensual focus will likely bring about disagreement and even conflict.

The purpose and objectives can, of course, be whatever the family wants them to be. For some families they are the continuation of a family business, with a focus on leadership succession, rather than benefit to the wider family. For some they're about preserving and growing the family's wealth more broadly and preventing fragmentation. Still others focus on how the wealth can benefit particular family members or generations, or society at large.

Setting out and communicating the purpose brings clarity which in turn reduces confusion and the perception of unfairness. Purpose that is built on a process that involves the family in its creation brings a sense of commitment and ownership to the outcomes. This should also help to make clear the different roles family members, now and into the future, can have in relation to the family's wealth with, most importantly, a clear set of expectations, responsibilities and accountabilities, boundaries and definitions in relation to those opportunities. Better that future family members should know what is expected of them, rather than see a set of expectations or entitlements as to what the family can do for them.

Yet experience shows that clarity and communication are often in short supply, with all the consequences that brings.

3.3 The needs of the family

There should be a clear articulation of what the family wealth is there to support, thereby helping family members to understand what they need to do for themselves. This can be very broad and may include the following as things that are either supported or not:

- **Welfare:**
  - retirement;

    - healthcare;
    - care for vulnerable family members; and/or
    - hardship.
- **Growth and development:**
    - education and skills;
    - employment;
    - financial advice; and/or
    - investment in enterprise or entrepreneurship.
- **Lifestyle:**
    - international travel; and/or
    - housing.

The statement should also articulate which members of the family the wealth is there to benefit, whether that be direct or indirect family members or the current, next or future generations. Better still, it should articulate the level of wealth intended for the family members or generations.

3.4 Benefits to society

If the purpose of the family's wealth is to benefit society more widely, then the vision for this should be articulated, as should the scale of resources to be applied as well as the time period over which this purpose is intended to operate.

3.5 The primary focus and vision of the family business

Where the family wealth is held in the form of a family business or businesses, a number of elements should be covered in the statement:

- Where the family anticipates its business focus to be. This might include how the family business can evolve, diversify or invest in new enterprises; or the circumstances in which it can be sold or exited, partially or as a whole.
- The balance between the financing needs of the business and the return that is generated for shareholders.
- Ownership concentration – whether, over time, ownership or shareholdings are likely to become fragmented or whether a structure should be developed to maintain a more centralised ownership strategy.

- The family's views on whether they should or can be led by family or non-family members.

3.6 The next generation(s)
Considerations regarding the next generation should cover two quite different perspectives. The first relates to the expected longevity of the family's wealth, while the second focuses on the levels of involvement or relationship the family are expected to have with the wealth. The latter might also touch on the succession philosophy as it relates to the stepping back or retirement of the senior generation.

We know that the growth in the size of a family is a potential natural cause of wealth fragmentation, so families have to decide how they wish to manage that risk. One way is to manage the extent of ownership concentration or spread of the wealth, laterally or vertically, between family members. Another is to potentially limit the distribution of the benefits from the wealth.

The second perspective – the level of family involvement – will reflect the family's views on whether and how members of the next generation might become involved in the business or the ownership or management of surplus wealth, as well as whether and by how much the next generation benefit from the wealth.

Clarity around what next-generation family members need to do to enable them to join the management of the family's wealth is very helpful in ensuring the family has the right skills for the future, as well as in challenging the sense of automatic entry.

3.7 The family values
The family vision statement should articulate the family's values. If the goals and objectives are about what the family wants to achieve, the values are about how they will go about achieving it. The values are, in effect, a statement of how the family will behave towards itself.

Importantly, the link between the what and the how should be harmonious and not dissonant.

A family's values should be relatively few in number, long term and non-negotiable. Values should act as both an inspiration for younger family members and a touchstone for the way the entire family, particularly the senior members, act. They should connect the generations and support the goals and objectives of the family and its wealth.

Family values are relatively easy to maintain and uphold when things are going well. Equally, they are easier to share and maintain when the family is smaller in terms of the number of generations involved and the breadth of family branches. More challenging is to uphold the family values in times of stress or difficulty. Yet it is precisely at these times that adherence to the family values is most important, as they can not only assist the family in navigating the difficulties but provide the framework within which communication and resolution can take place.

3.8 Summary

While the family vision statement should set out the goals, objectives and values succinctly, the process for determining what the statement contains is something that should not be rushed. Critical to this process is the involvement of a cross-section of the family, across and between the generations, working together to generate a vision that carries the shared support and commitment of the family and that will continue from one generation to the next.

Time needs to be set aside to ensuring that the family vision statement recognises the intended as well as the unintended consequences of its aims.

4. Elements of a family governance framework

4.1 Introduction

In this next section a brief has been created for each element of the governance structure. Each brief has been drafted with the following sections:

- an introduction to the governance framework element, providing a broad overview;
- an outline of the various philosophies or approaches that might be used in approaching the governance framework element, covering where applicable:
  - role;
  - membership;
  - chair; and
  - meetings and sundries; and
- key discussion points, focusing on some of the decisions or choices the family will need to make in approaching that element.

4.2 Family council

a. Introduction

The family council is one of the core components of a family governance framework. While the precise definition of the purpose and constitution of a family council can vary, it sits at the heart of the relationship between the family, the family business and/or wealth owners and the family business and/or wealth. A well-functioning family council aims to ensure unity, good governance and the avoidance of conflict between these three groups.

Its core purpose is to develop and strengthen the relationship between these three groups, whether in terms of planning, definition of roles and responsibilities, creation of policies or communication.

It is in effect the body charged with delivering the family vision while upholding the family values.

b. Role

Given the core purpose of the family council outlined above and a role that sits between three different groups, in practice the way in which a family council functions will depend on the extent to which it leans towards the family, the family business owners, or the family business.

Family forum: A family council that leans towards the family members will be more akin to a family assembly (see section 4.4 for a more detailed exposition of the role of a family assembly). Such a family council will be more concerned with the relationship between the family business and the wider family, and less with the day-to-day management of the family business. In such a family governance structure one might expect to see a larger number of non-shareholder family members, a largely external, non-family management board and/or a non-family chief executive of the family business.

Shareholder board: A family council that leans towards the family owners will be more concerned with the relationship between the interests of the owners and the performance of the family business. As, primarily, an ownership forum it might be titled a shareholder board, ownership council or supervisory board. One might expect to see a family assembly in this sort of family governance structure take care of the non-shareholder members of the family.

Family business board: Here, the family council combines the function of a shareholder board with coordination of the non-shareholder members of the family. It is more common with smaller family groups, where there is much greater overlap between the ownership and management groups of the business, and where there are few non-shareholder members of the family.

The approach the family takes in determining the role of the family council will be driven by the following factors:

- **The size of the family:** Very often it is the size of the family that will drive the role and purpose of the family council. For smaller families with a manageable number of family members it may be possible to combine the role of the family council and the family assembly.

- **The management of the family business:** Where there is a strong overlap between the owners and the directors/managers of the family business, there will be less need for a clear separation of the role of the family council. Conversely, where the directors/managers of the family business are not heavily drawn from within the family, there is likely to be a greater requirement for the family council to retain a role in driving the strategy and plans of the business and the oversight of management.
- **The range and complexity of the family business holdings:** Where the family has a range of business and asset holdings, a more focused family council is likely to be required.

The way in which the family's situation relates to the points set out above will need to be reflected in how the role of the family council is set out in the family protocols. It is important to recognise and ensure for more complex family governance arrangements that there is a clear distinction between the family council and the board of directors of the family business or the family council – they can complement each other, but they should not step into each other's territory.

Figure 5 on the next page indicates the range of topics, structures and governance relationships that a family council might cover.

c. Duties

A family council (where separately constituted from a family assembly) would be likely to have some or all of the following duties:

- to act as a forum for the ownership decisions of the family, keeping the family informed thereof and the board of the family business informed of the family's views about the company;
- to help the family speak with one voice about its goals and develop dynamic, caring shareholders;
- to agree and keep under review the family ownership philosophy for the family business and the vision and values, ensuring that such matters are discussed and lived by all. In particular to develop and maintain a strategy document for the family that covers the following:
    - a target return on equity;

Figure 5. Topics, structures and relationships covered by the family council

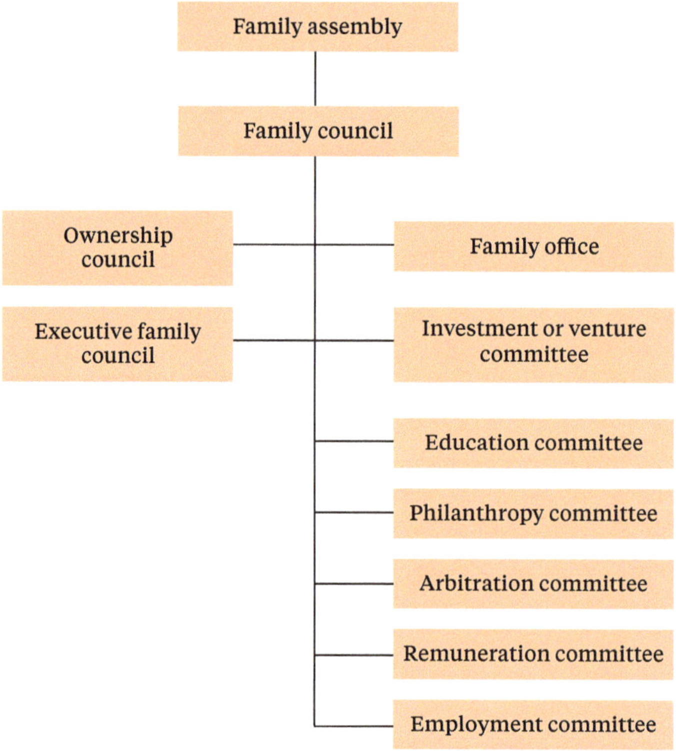

Source: Author.

    - a dividend policy; and
    - a policy for sale and purchase of shares, and any requirement for liquidity in the company to facilitate this;
- to manage the relationship between the family and the business, ensuring that there isn't too much interference, while also seeing that the family's goals are achieved;
- to develop and maintain family personnel and employment policies;
- to identify talent within the family to help it to endure, training and mentoring the next generation to achieve their full potential;
- to develop and maintain suitable vehicles for the ownership of the family business and assets;

- to encourage, support and assess new ideas;
- to develop the family's philanthropic commitments, and the policies necessary for their functioning and management;
- to implement processes to resolve conflict within the family and the family governance structures;
- to approve, review and maintain the family protocols;
- to agree, approve and keep under review the governance interface between family, shareholders and business;
- in relation to the family assembly:
  - to arrange and plan the family assembly meetings, social gatherings and other events to promote a unified family;
  - to discuss current business, ownership and family issues, keeping the family informed of these; and
  - to arrange educational events for the family in relation to the family business;
- in relation to the family business:
  - to develop plans and policies, which will need to be agreed with the board of the family business, that outline the involvement of the family with the family business, to include some or all of the following:
    - sign-off of strategic and business plans, and annual plans and forecasts;
    - setting performance benchmarks;
    - sign-off of audited accounts including, if relevant, the chair's statement;
    - sign-off of major expenditures;
    - approval of appointment of board directors and other major hiring decisions, as well as appointments of family members to other business or subsidiary boards;
    - approval of remuneration;
    - the level of delegated authorities; and/or
    - capital plans (including retentions and reserves), dividend policy, dividend payments, acquisitions and joint ventures, mergers and disposals;
  - to ensure the development of appropriate succession plans for family leadership of the family business. This should cover the development of the next generation of leaders in the

business, both family and non-family, as well as the development of the retirement or exit plans of the senior generation;
- to challenge the board of the family business, as appropriate, holding the board to account for financial performance, and measuring performance against the relevant goals, targets and benchmarks, according to the relevant reporting frequency;
- to receive information from the board relating to financial performance, including any relevant fiscal and environmental issues; and
- other key corporate issues, eg:
  - risk management policy and framework;
  - financial controls; and
  - audit.

Some families choose to have an executive family council. This is covered in section 4.3.

d. Membership

The key point in determining the composition of the family council is to ensure adequate representation of the family owners, with the size of the family being likely to drive its composition. For larger families, where to have all family owners at the family council is not possible, a branch-based representation model might be used. In this case each branch of the family will elect a representative to the family council.

The family will also need to determine if there are any other limits to be placed on membership. In different cultures and circumstances, membership limitations may include some or all of the following:
- direct bloodline descendants only;
- illegitimate or adopted children excluded; and/or
- in-laws excluded.

Provision should also be made for dealing with the following circumstances:
- the need for deputies where members of the council are unable to attend;

- illness or incapacity of council members;
- family owners or branches being unable to represent themselves at the council through being underage; and
- exclusion of family council members.

Given that the family council relates to the family ownership of the business, it would be unlikely that the family council would have non-family, non-owning, or non-executive directors as members.

e. Chair

The role of the chair of the family council is perhaps the most pivotal in the whole family governance arrangement and structure. The chair is responsible for:

- maintaining family unity;
- serving the interests of the family owners;
- being the driving force for achieving the family vision and upholding the family values;
- ensuring the rules are observed;
- ensuring fair dealings; and
- being in all likelihood the public face of the family.

A list of requirements – a profile – for the role of chair might be as follows:

- to maintain the respect of the family;
- to uphold family values;
- to be fair-minded;
- to maintain the vision, continuity and unity of the family;
- to achieve a balance between family and business interests;
- to possess strong leadership skills;
- to have the ability to manage the relationship with the board of the family business, ensuring the provision of leadership and direction and holding them to account;
- to possess strong communication skills;
- to be able to make provision for the development of the wider family and family members; and
- to have the ability to live the content and spirit of the protocols.

Provision needs to be made for the appointment of the chair. This would normally be by a vote of the members of the family council, with the chair being elected from their number. The following would normally be expected to be covered:

- limitations or exclusions on candidates;
- term length and renewal arrangements – it is good practice for the term length to be defined and for there to be the possibility of rotation of the chair role, although given that the chair is a representative of the owners within the family, one wouldn't expect to see a limit on the number of terms that can be served, or an upper age limit for the role holder;
- voting arrangements for electing the chair – the chair will usually be appointed by a simple majority of eligible votes, and the election process will need to cover the nomination arrangements and arrangements where there are more than two candidates;
- removal of the chair – provision should be made for the possibility of removing the chair, perhaps subject to a 75% majority vote of owners of the shares;
- provision for remuneration, if any; and
- arrangements for an alternate chair in the absence of the chair from a meeting.

f. Meetings and sundries

Upholding the rule of the majority: Given the commitment to the continuity of the family, the family protocols and family governance mechanisms work on the basis of transparency and fairness. Respect for the rules and decisions taken are therefore crucial, particularly with regard to those in the minority on a given decision. This also needs to be carried through by all in terms of implementing decisions taken.

Voting: Given the commitment to unity and continuity, building a sense of teamwork, trust and pride in what the family and business are aiming to achieve is important. The family council should therefore seek to promote consensus-based decision making; an appreciation for the expression of, and a willingness to hear, different perspectives and points of view; and a resolve not to avoid conflict at the expense of openness and transparency.

Notwithstanding the above, the family council needs to have in place a mechanism for reaching decisions where consensus cannot be reached and to avoid deadlock.

Voting rules need to be developed. They can vary, from a system based on one person, one vote through to a voting system where each council member votes the size of their shareholding.

Voting thresholds need to be set: normally a simple majority for ordinary resolutions and a 75% majority for special resolutions. The following items are often subject to a special resolution and thus a 75% majority:

- reserved decisions in relation to the family business, eg:
  - agreeing an IPO or sale of the business or a part thereof;
  - raising capital for the business; or
  - requiring a family member to exit;
- removing the chair or a family council member from office;
- suspending or excluding a family member; and
- changes to the family governance protocols where a special resolution is required.

Issues not requiring a special resolution would be dealt with as ordinary resolutions.

Other issues in relation to voting that should be covered include:

- proxy voting mechanisms; and
- the procedure by which issues have to be raised before a vote can be taken, thereby ensuring an orderly flow of business and ensuring all members of the council are aware of proceedings.

Proceedings: Given the central role of the family council in the governance of the family and business, a high degree of importance must be given to its smooth operation and working, and this relates as much to the processes that surround the meetings of the council as to the meetings themselves.

The governance framework should therefore contain provisions in respect of the following:

- meeting frequency;
- the need for an AGM;
- notice of meetings;
- agenda notification and circulation;
- the process for raising agenda items;
- quorum;
- the process for extraordinary meetings;
- minutes;
- sub-committees; and
- communication.

KEY POINTS

The key points for discussion by family members with regard to the family council are as follows:

The role of the family council: Sections 4.2 b. and c. above set out in some detail the potential roles and duties of a family council.

While it is a body that faces off to the family, perhaps most critical is understanding that the family council plays a different role to that of the board of directors in relation to the family business. In this regard, the following issues are key:

- whether the family council is, in effect, the shareholder board;
- the retained powers of the family council;
- the strategic direction given to the board of the family business;
- the expectations in terms of results set by the family council;
- family leadership succession; and
- the relationship between the two bodies in terms of accountability.

Other issues to consider include:

- the size of the family, and the level of responsibilities to reside with the family council;
- the relationship with the family assembly (if there is one); and
- the relationship with the executive family council (if there is one).

Decision making, voting and the rule of the majority: Given the pivotal role played by the family council, it is critical that these areas are discussed and the procedures clearly set out – in a united family one would hope that most decisions will be reached by consensus, but this will not always be the case. There is potential for certain manoeuvres to bring about deadlock, and rules should be put in place to ensure that this does not happen, or that if it does, there is a mechanism for resolution.

While the concept of rule of the majority is largely taken for granted, it is important for families to recognise that taken together, this rule and the concept of representation in line with the value of shares held are the basics that underpin decision making in a family council.

Openness and transparency: Within a family who have agreed to continue to work together, openness and transparency are key. The standards to be reached are higher than would be encountered in normal commercial business relationships.

The chair: The role of chair is pivotal in the family governance structure. Consequently, care needs to be taken in the way in which the role is crafted and how the role profile is drawn up. After all, the chair can, subject to re-election, be in position for a long time.

Careful thought needs to be given to whether the chair of the family council should also be the chair of the board of directors of the family business. There is no reason why one individual shouldn't hold both positions; however, it will concentrate powers and the issues raised will need to be thought through properly. Such concentration of power might be acceptable, even attractive, in the early stages of the development of a family governance system, or for families in a first- or second-generation position. For families that have developed through multiple generations, however, a separation or balance of powers might be more appropriate.

Equally, the way the family council chair role is defined will be different if the senior management positions of the family business are held by non-family executives.

4.3 Executive family council

a. Introduction

An executive family council is sometimes part of the family governance architecture. It may be referred to as the 'council of elders' or 'council of seniors'. It is likely to be encountered more often in cultures that place a high value on the role of the elder generation.

More broadly, the engagement and support of the senior generation is likely to be very important to the functioning and legitimacy of a family council, particularly where the senior generation includes the founder. Thus, the core purpose of an executive family council is to act as the forum where the founder or selected members of the senior generation are specifically engaged in the family governance process.

b. Role

An executive family council is more likely to be encountered in situations where the founder, or sufficient numbers of the senior generation, are not represented on the family council or where certain powers or decisions are retained by the founder or senior generation. The precise role of an executive family council will depend on the reasons for its establishment; specifically, whether it is a forum for one or more of the following:

- communicating with the founder or senior generation, particularly where the senior generation have strong views on the future of the family business or are finding it difficult to relinquish control, or where the generational transition or succession remains unclear;
- obtaining guidance from the founder or senior generation;
- discussing key issues or decisions by the main representatives in the family governance architecture, who come together for that purpose; or
- consulting with the founder or senior generation on issues of governance in which they retain a power of veto.

The role of the executive family council should be set out clearly in the family governance framework and should be referenced in the role definition of the body or bodies to which it relates; for example, if it relates to the family council, then its role, and any powers given to it, should be defined in the section setting out the duties of the family council. This should ensure that overlap and confusion of roles is kept to a minimum.

Equally, it is an important requirement that the executive family council communicates clearly back into the family governance architecture, for example to family council meetings.

c. Membership

The executive family council's membership should reflect its powers and role. Where it is a body focused on engaging the founder, it may be that the membership includes a number of defined role holders: for example, the founder, the chair of the family council and the chair of the board of directors of the family business. For such additional role holders, a decision needs to be taken about whether they are full members or attendees.

Alternatively, if it is to be a representative body of the senior generation, its members may be elected by and from the senior generation.

d. Chair

One member will be elected chair – normally the founder, the most senior member of the family or the member with the largest shareholding.

KEY POINTS

The key discussion points regarding the executive family council are likely to be:

- the nature and scope of any retained powers or powers of veto;
- the influencing powers of the founder; and
- whether the council has a defined life linked to the lifetime of the founder or the senior generation.

"Family assemblies can play a role in helping to avoid and defuse misunderstandings, disagreement and conflict between family members because of oft-perceived inequality of access to information, treatment or resources."

4.4 Family assembly

a. Introduction

The family assembly is a representative body for all members of the family to come together to maintain wider family unity and togetherness and to uphold the family values.

The assembly is particularly important for those branches and members of the family that do not hold shares. It should enable the wider family to gain a better understanding of the business of the family and the family business, and to keep abreast of developments. It might provide the platform for the introduction of next-generation members of the wider family to become engaged with the family business and see it as a future career for themselves. It will also be likely to underpin the social development of the family.

The family assembly is to some degree an optional body in family governance architecture and is likely to reflect, on the one hand, the size and spread of a family, and on the other the role of the family council. For larger and multi-generational families, particularly where many family members are not shareholders, a family assembly is likely to play an important role in the family governance architecture.

It also plays a role in developing a sense of accountability to the wider family by those who work in the business or are shareholders in the family business, bearing in mind the wider family's name and reputation, lifestyle and livelihood may depend on the success of the family business.

The family assembly should be designed and operated with a view to maximising the participation and attendance of family members. Family assemblies can play a role in helping to avoid and defuse misunderstandings, disagreement and conflict between family members because of oft-perceived inequality of access to information, treatment or resources. Social activity is often combined with business and family-focused discussions.

b. Role

The family assembly's scope and role include the following:

- It should meet with sufficient frequency to facilitate good communication within the family.
- Its meetings are an opportunity for everyone to learn about and contribute to business and family developments, and to discuss opportunities as well as the health and future of the family.
- It should be responsible for sharing and maintaining the vision and values of the family.
- It will hear about the progress the business is making, its strategic direction and any changes to the business.
- It might have an annual family conference or retreat with all family members attending. This meeting of the whole family will aim to enhance family members' understanding and respect for the personal, business and family issues that bind the family together.
- Its meetings are a way for younger family members to learn about the history, values and traditions of the family as well as the business issues and opportunities. In this context, the senior family members are responsible for teaching the younger family members the responsibilities of ownership.
- It will have a focus on improving the standard and quality of the lives of the family members, and in particular on the care required for any family member who has particular needs.
- It might be a forum for discussion of revisions to the family constitution.

c. Membership

Given the focus on learning about the business and building relationships, typically all family members, spouses and children will be invited to be part of the family assembly.

There is usually a minimum age requirement that can be defined in a number of ways – perhaps over a certain age or participation in at least six months of secondary education.

d. Chair

While the chair of the family assembly might be elected by the family assembly or appointed by the founder, what is more important is that the chair is a widely respected member of the family. Provision should be made for the role of chair to be rotated periodically, but this would not be too often, as length of tenure here would be important to maintaining consistency.

e. Meetings and proceedings

While meetings and proceedings of the family assembly can vary from formal to informal, it is important to ensure that the agenda focuses on delivering the value-add demanded of the assembly.

KEY POINTS

The following points are likely to need consideration in the formation of a family assembly:

- age limits for family members;
- the issues, if any, on which the input or views of the family assembly are required, for example:
  - family member employment policies;
  - remuneration policies;
  - arbitration or family conflict policies;
  - reputation management policies;
  - education funding;
  - helping the needy in the family; and
  - philanthropy;
- the extent to which the family assembly will test the strength of the family ties, and the actual level of support for the vision and values of the family; and
- which costs will be covered by the family, and which by individual family members.

4.5 Family branch assemblies

a. Introduction

These are included where the family is either large enough to require being managed, from a family ownership perspective, on the basis of family branch representation, or where the family does not wish the ownership of the core of the business assets to be fragmented widely as ensuing generations become involved in the governance of the business and family.

Family branch assemblies are the bodies established for each family branch that make the decisions for their representatives on the family ownership decision-making bodies – most likely the family council or the family business holding company board.

Family branch assemblies do not, ordinarily, exist for any other activities.

b. Role

Each family branch assembly acts like a microcosm of the wider family council in that it is the body representing the ownership of that branch's shareholding in the family business and assets.

As an ownership body itself, the family branch assembly should ideally also have a legal structure, and this ownership structure will largely drive the decisions taken by the branch assembly, although this should be decided explicitly.

The family branch assembly will meet to decide how to vote the family branch shareholding in decisions to be taken in the overarching family council. Its activities, meetings and decisions will therefore need to be undertaken in a timely fashion to allow adequate time for, on the one hand, consideration of the issues on which it is required to express its view and, on the other, consideration of the issues in a manner that does not unnecessarily hold up the timely execution of the business of the family council.

Family branch assemblies can take the form of either informal groupings governed by the rules, or incorporated entities – for example, LLCs or foundations.

Family branch assemblies should be fully engaged with, and

supportive of, the family vision and values; and as a general point, the family governance framework should flow consistently through all the various layers of bodies that exist, including branch assemblies. This consistency will allow the timely conduct of family business without unnecessary delays or loopholes.

c. Membership

Membership will normally be restricted to the owners of the family branch shareholding in the family business and assets.

d. Chair

A member of the branch assembly will be elected chair, but will generally be the senior member of that branch of the family.

e. Meetings and sundries

Meetings will take place at appropriate intervals to fit with the business timetable of the overarching family council.

One member of the family branch assembly will need to be appointed to represent the branch assembly at the family council.

KEY POINTS

The following points will need to be discussed in relation to family branch assemblies:

Rationale and implications: Family branch assemblies will typically appear in a family governance framework once the family has expanded to the point where the third generation (and possibly beyond) are fully and actively involved in the governance of the family and the family business, but where the generation one level higher in the family structure do not believe that ownership of the family business should be fragmented beyond the number of family members in their own generation. This will typically mean that ownership of the family business is split between two and seven owners, and that fragmentation will not go any further as the family expands.

Such a strategy can avoid the situation where the core family assets end up being owned by an ever-widening number of shareholders, with all the practical difficulties that brings. However, introducing family branch assemblies brings a different set of organisational challenges in terms of coordinating the branches.

One issue that can arise is that families can feel uncomfortable when the dilution of ownership is affected by the number of children in each branch. Say, for example, there are three family branches, and each has a different number of children in the next generation. There could well be disharmony based on the uneven dilution of shares. This problem is largely unavoidable but it does need to be thought about and explained to the family.

Rules of engagement: If the family council is composed of representatives from the family branches, then clear rules need to be determined not only for the functioning of the family council, but also for the extent to which discretion around the voting powers of the family branches is delegated to the branch representative. If these rules are not made clear then there may be severe difficulties in organising the proceedings of the family council and managing the expectations of the family branch assembly members. Equally, it is not unusual for competition to break out between the branches when it comes to which branch family members hold key positions. Checks, controls and counterbalances need to be discussed.

Changes over time: Introducing family branch assemblies does not mean that ownership of the core family assets or the family branch shareholdings cannot change over time. The family governance framework will typically be structured to include provisions for family branches to acquire and sell some or all of their shareholding in the core family assets to other family branches, and for family branch members to acquire and sell some portion of their ownership of the family branch shareholding. There may also be provisions that prevent one branch acquiring holdings above a certain percentage or a particular branch acquiring a controlling stake.

Distancing of family members from the family business: Family branches may have the effect of distancing family members from the family business, as primary involvement rests with the branch representative. The family members will still, hopefully, enjoy distributions, although care needs to be taken to ensure this doesn't become a dependency. Thought needs to be given to the ways in which this can be counterbalanced, with the family assembly playing a key role.

4.6 Family office

a. Introduction

While the term 'family office' is widely seen in family governance structures, it lacks a precise definition. A family office can come in different forms and cover a very wide variety of activities. In broad terms it can be expected to support a family through the organisation, administration, management and maintenance of its wealth and affairs. Under a narrower definition, a family office might be responsible for the management of the family's financial assets, where the family wishes to maintain a high degree of control over the management of those assets.

By their nature, the activities of the family office include matters and information that are very personal and sensitive to individual members of the family and to the family as a whole. The approach to the development of a family office therefore requires careful consideration.

Regardless of the approach pursued and the range of activities to be scoped, the establishment of a family office typically involves delegating activities regarding the wealth and affairs of the family to outside parties, whether individuals or institutional providers of services. It is, therefore, crucial that the family maintains close control of the governance of the family office. The family will need to:

- establish strategic goals and objectives for the activities undertaken;
- create a clear mandate and control framework for the delegation of tasks; and

- monitor closely the activities of, and results achieved by, the family office.

b. Types of family office

Broadly speaking, family offices can be split into three types:

Single family office: This is a dedicated entity looking after the affairs of a single family. If an SFO is to provide the full suite of family office functions to a family, the level of wealth would need to be significant to justify the costs.

Multi-family office: An MFO will manage the affairs of several families, who are unlikely to be connected to each other. MFOs can be both private, often having started their life as an SFO, or commercial, having been established by professionals drawn from the wealth, investment management, legal and accounting industries. MFOs typically look to provide a wide range, if not all, of the functions of a family office, using economies of scale to spread the workload and lower the costs of providing the different services.

Virtual family office: A VFO seeks to provide the benefits of a family office through outsourcing the requirements to external consultants, professionals and service providers. This route avoids the need to set up a dedicated organisation and allows for a pick and mix approach to the scope of services. A family setting up a VFO still requires a coordination and management function.

Whichever of the above options a family selects, consideration will need to be given to the form, structure and governance of the family office entity and the way it fits with the broader structure and governance of the family's wealth and affairs.

c. Scope of activities

Family offices can provide a very wide range of functions, as follows:

- **Investment management:**
  - investment objectives and investment philosophy;
  - risk profiling;

  - strategic and tactical asset allocation;
  - manager selection;
  - stock selection;
  - manager monitoring;
  - liquidity management;
  - dealing and trade settlement;
  - benchmarking;
  - performance analysis and reporting;
  - risk analysis, management and reporting;
  - custody management;
  - consolidated reporting of all assets; and
  - compliance and regulatory reporting.
- **Advisory functions:**
  - tax, legal, regulatory and compliance;
  - estate planning;
  - philanthropy;
  - financial planning, structuring and budgeting;
  - access to banking and trust services;
  - risk management and insurance; and
  - physical, IT and data security.
- **Inter-generational planning:**
  - training; and
  - education.
- **Governance:**
  - family office oversight and management;
  - support for family council, family assembly and philanthropy matters; and
  - staffing decisions.
- **Administrative functions:**
  - education;
  - record keeping and data management;
  - expense management and bill paying;
  - travel and lifestyle;
  - secretarial support;
  - personnel;
  - real estate and other property management;
  - household and domestic arrangements;

- risk and reputation management (PR, social media, physical and data security, insurance, asset protection, disaster recovery, social media and confidentiality);
- audit;
- club memberships;
- property, art and wine;
- yacht and private jet management; and
- disaster recovery.

d. Role

The formation of a family office is often associated with one or more of the following factors:

- a significant increase in the level of financial assets owned by a family;
- a desire by the family to exercise a greater degree of control over the management of its financial assets or affairs; or
- a wish to provide for dedicated and separate provision of services previously provided by a family-owned operating company.

While these are the most common drivers, the following may also be relevant:

- a desire to manage the family wealth/assets together, based on shared interests, necessitating a more centralised model for the delivery of services;
- a need for closer governance and/or management arrangements, including maximising the alignment of interests between the family and any advisers;
- a focus on continuity of wealth into the next generation; and
- a desire to achieve higher levels of returns and/or closer management of risk.

e. Cost

The issue of cost needs to be considered carefully as it can vary quite significantly according to the range of activities within the family office's scope. The costs of an in-house family office need to be compared to the alternatives and justified in terms of the impact of the costs on the investment return generated. It is not unusual to see a minimum assets under management (AUM) figure in the region of $250m required to justify a fully in-house single family office.

f. Expertise, time and interest

Family expertise, time and interest also need to be assessed in determining the structure of a family office. Any form of family office requires the family or family members to have an adequate degree of expertise to either manage activities directly themselves or oversee the management of certain activities. Where the support and activities required are to be provided via some form of in-house family office, then an adequate commitment of time and interest will be required to manage the family office functions.

g. Trust and management of risk

The creation of a family office for the purpose of managing the financial assets and affairs of a family still requires a degree of separation between the ownership and the management of the family's financial assets and affairs. The precise nature and degree of this separation of powers need to be fully assessed, the implications thought through and any resulting arrangements with, and between, family members and family office staff carefully defined and managed.

A family office involves the investment of a significant degree of trust in the family office staff. The risks inherent in this need to be identified and proper boundaries, control and oversight established. The risks need to be managed and/or mitigated through an appropriate set of risk management practices and arrangements.

h. In-house or external

Whether to create a family office based on in-house or external capabilities is not an all or nothing choice. For each of the services within the scope of the family office an assessment needs to be made as to which route to follow. A number of factors will drive the in-house/external choice.

Core or satellite capability requirement: A clear understanding of the core purpose(s) of the family office will provide an initial outline of the services that are most likely to require in-house expertise, whether that

"Family offices are, ordinarily, relatively small entities in staffing terms. In-house hiring decisions require careful consideration to ensure that the cost is justified by sufficient demand for the services and that, where an in-house provision decision is made, there is sufficient depth of expertise to ensure resilience of service delivery by the family office staff."

be from a family member(s), through oversight of the capability or taking it on directly, or a family office resource to deliver the capability from outside the family. Service requirements that are not core are most likely to be externally sourced.

Scale and depth of the demand: Family offices are, ordinarily, relatively small entities in staffing terms. In-house hiring decisions require careful consideration to ensure that the cost is justified by sufficient demand for the services and that, where an in-house provision decision is made, there is sufficient depth of expertise to ensure resilience of service delivery by the family office staff. Otherwise, key person risk will arise and, equally, longer-term succession and continuity might be a problem.

These risks are likely to be exacerbated where the family office staff operate in areas of significant complexity requiring experienced and, consequently, expensive resources. But the risks will be lower for regular, repetitive and less complex activities.

Level of expertise: Where the level of expertise required is very specialist, unless there is sufficient demand across the family to warrant an in-house capability, then external sourcing is likely to be the right option. Furthermore, for deeply specialist areas there is likely to be a requirement for ongoing support, which a small in-house capability is unlikely to be able to provide. An external sourcing route will also tend to ensure that the service capability stays up to date with external best practice and in line with regulatory or legal requirements.

Cost dynamics: Clearly, cost is going to be an important factor. Comparison of the various options, including sourcing bundled capabilities from external providers, is going to be really important to help reach a clear understanding of the costs involved in running a family office. This is only going to be possible once a clear scoping of the intended activities of the family office has been drawn up.

Conflicts of interest: A proper assessment of principal/agency issues needs to be undertaken to understand how and where interests are either aligned or in conflict. A principal/agency problem can occur in either the in-house or the external family office model. Risk management and controls will need to be put in place to deal with this. The scale and nature of the issue will determine how it affects the in-house or external sourcing of capability.

Privacy: Where there is a very strong requirement for privacy and confidentiality in respect of a particular capability requirement, then an in-house route is likely to be more suitable.

The advantages of a family office can include flexibility, bespoke design and structure, and a choice of the degree of involvement in and control over the activities of the family office. These have to be set against the potential disadvantages which, beyond the issue of cost, can include the sourcing, reward, motivation, management and retention of a small group of family office staff, with the potential for real key person risk; needing to create and manage an appropriate risk management framework, as reliance cannot be placed on the processes and controls brought by external providers; and finally maintaining family harmony when the functions of the family office are being led, if not performed, by family members.

i. Establishing a family office

The process for establishing a family office should follow a series of structured steps, as below.

Initial assessment: The first stage is to conduct a high-level assessment of what the family is trying to achieve. This should capture the following, as a minimum:

- **Goal:** This is the overarching goal that the family has for setting up a family office, for example:
  The family has agreed to establish a family office to provide skilled and dedicated resources to meet the needs of all family members. This will alleviate the demands placed on employees of the family business to provide private support to family members.
- **Objectives:** This refers to the specific objectives that sit beneath the overall goal. These should provide a sense of the functional

capabilities required by the family, but more importantly a sense of what those capabilities are being designed to achieve. As part of this, the nature and extent of the assets to be managed by the family office should be assessed, as this will be critical in determining the management capabilities required.

- **Capability:** An assessment needs to be made of the capability that exists within the family to either undertake activities in the family office or be part of its governance and control structure. It is not unusual for a family, prior to the establishment of a family office, to have relied on resources within the family business. An assessment should be made of that capability and the possibility of some or all of those resources becoming part of the family office capability.
- **Coverage:** This part of the exercise should establish how many family members wish to be covered by the family office, and for which activities in particular. Ultimately the costs of the family office have to be borne by the family members, and this exercise should test the extent to which family members are going to be prepared to pay for the services delivered by the family office.
- **Risk:** An initial risk assessment should be undertaken to identify the key areas of risk for the family in setting up a family office, as well as the areas of risk likely to be present within the family office once established. Key headings are likely to include:
  - investment risk (including return, liquidity and volatility risks, and the risks associated with external asset managers);
  - governance risk (including risks associated with levels of competence and experience, controls and oversight, and alignment of interests);
  - security risk (including counterparty, custody, insurance, data, physical and people risks); and
  - political, legal and regulatory risks.

In light of the outcome of the assessment of the above considerations, the family should be able determine, at a high level, whether and what sort of family office is viable for them. The critical issue in this determination will be the level of capability that exists within the family or family business.

Outline design: With the initial assessment complete, the next stage is to create an outline design for the family office, including the following:

- **Key functions:** The outline design of the family office will list the key functions that the family office will provide, under the headings described in section c. above and in Table 5 on the next page.
- **Jurisdiction:** A jurisdiction will need to be selected for the family office. While legal and tax considerations are often cited as the key ones for the choice of location, it is equally, if not more, important to assess what is a suitable location from the perspectives of control, oversight and operation. Proximity, for these purposes, to the key members of the family is likely to be very important, particularly where there is a high level of in-house service provision.

  Legal and taxation considerations will need to be assessed in light of the key functions of the family office. Where the family office requires the establishment of a number of different legal entities, clearly these considerations will need to be applied to all of them. Along with the overall assessment from a legal and tax perspective, the choice of jurisdiction should take into account the locations of the family members covered by the family office. Where investment management functions are taken on by the family office, the regulatory environment within the legal jurisdiction will be important. Registration and licences are typically required for investment management functions.
- **Structure:** The initial assessment will have looked at the objectives and key services required of the family office by the family. It will also have assessed the family's capability to either manage or oversee the functions of the family office, and the scale of demand from family members for the family office functions.

  The balance as between these factors will provide a good starting point regarding the likely structure of the family office – from a full-function family office to a more focused investment office and from in-house to outsourced. While it's something of a generalisation, an in-house family office will require either strong family capability or strong family oversight of hired staff.

Table 5. Outline design of the family office

Investment	Advisory	Inter-generational	Governance	Administration
Investment objectives and philosophy	Tax	Next-generation training	Family council and family assembly coordination and management	Schooling and university
Risk tolerance profiling	Legal	Education	Philanthropy management	Record keeping and data management
Strategic and tactical asset allocation	Regulatory and compliance		Staff management	Expense management and bill paying
Manager selection	Estate planning			Travel and lifestyle
Stock selection	Philanthropy			Secretarial support
Manager monitoring	Financial planning			Personnel
Liquidity management	Budgeting			Real estate and other property management
Deal and trade settlement	Wealth structuring			Household and domestic arrangements
Benchmarking	Banking and trust services			Risk and reputation management
Performance analysis and reporting	Risk management			Insurance
Risk analysis	Insurance			Audit
Management reporting	Physical, IT and data security			Club memberships
Custody management				Disaster recovery
Consolidated reporting				
Compliance and regulatory reporting				

The absence of either of these mean that outsourcing of many of the requirements is likely, although it has to be recognised that such arrangements need to be managed carefully.

Full-function family office: Set out in Figure 6 is a staffing model for a full-function in-house family office derived from the list of functions set out in section c. above. The precise design will be a variation on this model, with the breadth and number of staff needing to be employed dependent upon the extent to which the services are provided in-house or through outsourced arrangements. Importantly, even where services are outsourced, staff will be required to manage the outsourced service providers.

Figure 6. Full-function family office model

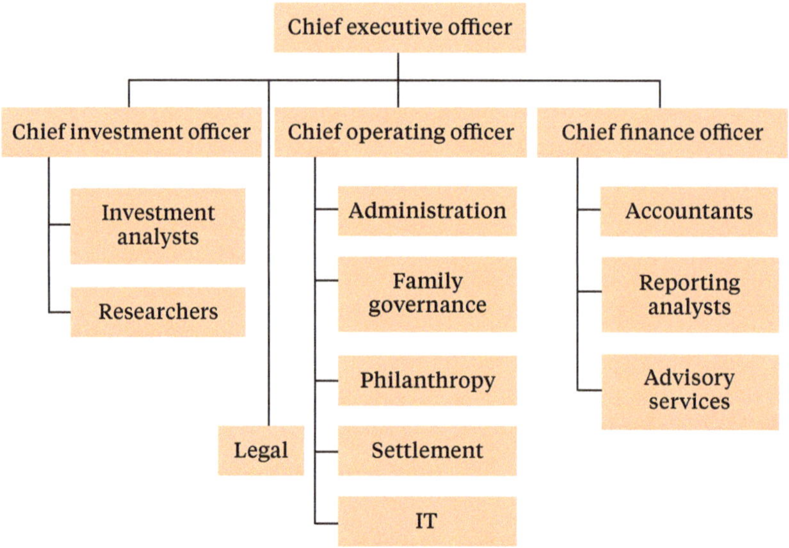

Source: Author.

Where the full range of functions of a family office is provided, it affords the possibility of organising the office in a way that allows for a full separation of duties to avoid either conflicts of interest, or concentration of tasks with inadequate separation of controls and management of risk. The natural separation of the investment function under the CIO, the finance and reporting function under the CFO and the administration and settlement functions under the COO, is helpful in this regard.

Where a family office doesn't have sufficient scale for this natural separation of duties, additional controls and/or oversight will need to be added.

Family investment office: The core role of a family office is often cited as the investment management function. Where this is the only or the main function of the family office, the organisation chart may look like that shown in Figure 7, with the most senior role being chief investment officer, with teams beneath the CIO covering investment analysis and research; administration and settlement; and finance and reporting. Where such a structure is adopted, careful thought will need to be given to the reporting line and arrangements for the CIO as well as the control arrangements required.

Figure 7. Family investment office model – option 1

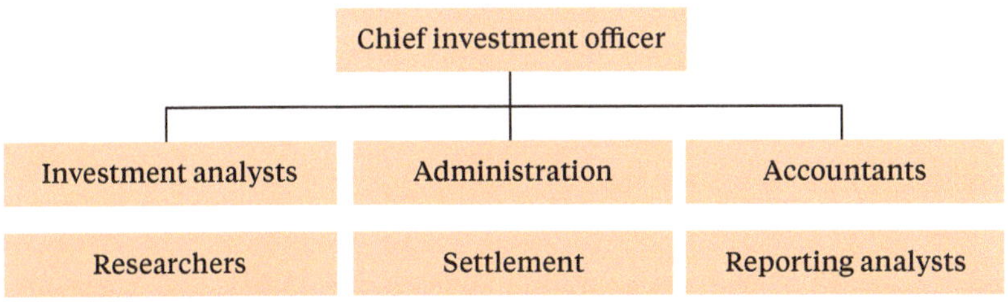

Source: Author.

Another option, shown in Figure 8, is for the family investment office to have only an advisory role in relation to the family investments, with execution and reporting of the investment management activities carried out by the management of the family investment ownership vehicle or by external asset managers. While this approach has the advantage of separating the investment advice from the execution and reporting of the investment management strategies, it does bring an additional layer of complexity to the family investment office set-up.

Figure 8. Family investment office model – option 2

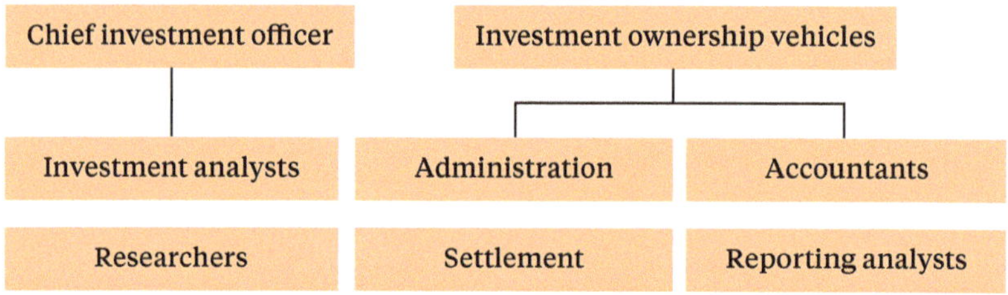

Source: Author.

With the focus of the family investment office on investment management activities, it may be that the office is incorporated as a separate body from the other, more administrative, functions of the family office due the increased level of compliance and regulations that apply to investment management functions.

Clearly, however the functions of the family office are organised, there needs to be adequate management and oversight.

- **Risk management:** Before moving to the detailed design stage, the initial risk assessment should be revisited and updated, under the same key headings, namely:
  - investment risk (including return, liquidity and volatility risks, and the risks associated with external asset managers);
  - governance risk (including risks associated with levels of competence and experience, controls and oversight, and alignment of interests);
  - security risk (including counterparty, custody, insurance, data, physical and people risks); and
  - political, legal and regulatory risks.

Detailed design: With an outline design established, the next stage is to define in detail how it will operate.

- **Family offices and the investment management process:** Table 6 sets out the range of investment management functions that a family office is likely to have to oversee or undertake where it is established for investment management purposes. The particular bodies and persons that have been selected are for illustrative purposes only, and reflect a situation where there is an in-house CIO and investment team, reporting to a family office investment board that in turn reports to the family council.

Table 6. Investment management functions

Function	Primary decision maker	Control function	Reporting line entity
Investment objectives and philosophy	Family council	N/A	N/A
Risk profiling	Family council	N/A	N/A
Strategic asset allocation	Family office investment board	External investment consultant	Family council
Tactical asset allocation	Internal investment team	Investment policy limits	Family office investment board
Manager selection	Internal investment team	Investment policy limits	Family office investment board
Stock selection	Internal investment team	Investment policy limits	Family office investment board
Manager monitoring	Internal investment team	Investment objectives and benchmarks	Family office investment board
Liquidity management	Internal investment team	Investment policy limits	Family office investment board
Deal and trade settlement	Global custodian	Family office finance function	Family office investment board

continued on next page

Function	Primary decision maker	Control function	Reporting line entity
Benchmarking	Internal investment team	Family office finance function	Family office investment board
Performance analysis and reporting	Internal investment team	Family office finance function	Family office investment board & family council
Risk analysis	Internal investment team	Family office finance function	Family office investment board
Management reporting	Family office finance function	Family office investment board	Family council
Custody management	Global custodian	Family office investment board	Family office investment board
Compliance and regulatory reporting	Family office finance function	Family office investment board	Family office investment board
Consolidated reporting	Family office finance function	Family office investment board	Family council

- **Policies and procedures:** Each function in Table 6 should be supported by a detailed policy and set of procedures. This will establish the precise framework within which each of the functions operates, including details of the roles responsible for decisions, the limits on decisions and decision makers, and the escalation procedures. The policy and procedures framework is designed to ensure that the investment process operates in line with the family objectives and avoids decision making that is out of line with the objectives, or outside established limits or parameters. The policies and procedures also provide the framework against which the controls can take place and many of the risks can be managed.

- **Infrastructure:** There are two aspects to the infrastructure that need to be considered – staff and systems:
  - **Staff:** There are several key issues to consider when building the staff capability for a family investment office which, importantly, need to be seen in the context of a family investment office often being a small establishment. These include:
    - **Knowledge and experience:** Specific investment knowledge and experience relevant to the operations of the family investment office are essential. This could mean knowledge of the asset classes into which the family investment office is going to invest; the types of function or entity the individual is going to be managing; or the type of controls or risks that need to be managed. Delegation or outsourcing of a function to an external provider doesn't remove the requirement to manage the process and the risks associated with it.
    - **Oversight:** Small teams of people often mean that individuals can end up with a wider role scope as compared to what might be the case in larger organisations, and this often occurs unwittingly. It is important that all roles are reviewed to ensure that there is adequate separation of duties and oversight of tasks undertaken.
  - **Systems:** Systems are likely to be required for the following functions:
    - custody;
    - consolidated reporting;
    - trading and portfolio management;
    - risk management and reporting;
    - financial and management accounting; and
    - tax reporting.
- **Risk assessment:** A final, detailed, risk assessment review should be undertaken, with particular emphasis on governance risk, including risks associated with levels of competence and experience, controls and oversight, and alignment of interests.

j. Governance and oversight

The issue of governance and oversight of a family office needs to be considered at two levels. The first is at the level of the body within the family governance framework to which the family office reports – typically the family council; the second is at the level of the legal entity of the family office.

In assessing the level of oversight required, the following key factors should be taken into account:

Family member experience and involvement: Where a family has extensive and widely spread experience in the areas to be covered by the family office, it makes sense that this should be leveraged through the governance structure, and would likely result in a number of family members being appointed to the family office controlling body (the family office board or committee). This should provide the family council with a good degree of comfort in the area of oversight of the family office, assuming that proper systems are put in place within the family office.

Where a family has less experience in this area, or the experience is concentrated in one individual, and the family wishes to bolster oversight within the family office, it can appoint external advisers/experts to the family office controlling body. Some families choose to appoint an external person as chair of the family office controlling body, others to appoint external directors to the family office controlling body, to bring an appropriate degree of independence and expertise into the relationship between family members and the management team of the family office.

Delegation and concentration of powers: It is up to the family council to determine the level of delegation of powers to the family office. It can impose limits on (or indeed retain decision-making control in relation to) the range of powers, decision making and reporting. Such limitations or retained powers will be set out in the governing document of the family office.

Nature of the investments: The family office may potentially undertake a very wide range of investments, depending on the history and nature of the family's wealth and its wealth objectives for the future. The family council will need to satisfy itself that it has created adequate oversight and governance relevant to the range of possible investments the family office might make. The following list is by no means exhaustive:

- shares;
- bonds;
- active, passive and hedge funds;
- land and property;
- commodities;
- structured investment instruments;
- hedging;
- private equity; and
- new ventures.

k. Family office board (or family office committee)

Where the family office is in the legal form of a limited company there will need to be a board. For other legal entity forms, the body with direct control of the family office might be a family office committee. The precise nature and shape of the family office board will depend on the factors set out in the preceding section, and will be set out in a family office charter or equivalent governing document for the family office entity. It is to be expected that a number of family members, who also sit on the family council, will be members of this body, and one of their number may be elected to the role of chair (but see the next section on the appointment of the chair).

The family office board needs to be able to access the people and information required to allow it to perform its role. And where external services are sourced, because these are likely to be via the family office the board will require the powers and expertise to procure and manage these relationships.

l. Chair

While the choice of a chair should be informed by and be appropriate to the purpose and function of the family office, consideration should also be given to whether the chair should be a family member or a non-family member. One approach is to recruit a non-family member as chair where the CEO/CIO is a family member, and vice versa, thereby providing an additional level of objectivity to the oversight.

KEY POINTS

At a high level the following points regarding the family office will need to be discussed:

Need: The starting point for discussion within a family about a family office is establishing whether there is a real need for one, and if so, articulating what those needs are. If a family office is to be established, there has to be a recognition that this is in line with a long-term view of the management of the family's financial assets and/or affairs and that the family office will be managed as part of the family governance infrastructure. The need for a family office should be underpinned by a very strong desire to closely align the family's shared purpose, vision and values (with an appropriately long-term view) with the necessary financial and investment management expertise.

Clear requirements and objectives should be identified for the family office that are over and above those that can be provided through bilateral relationships with a portfolio of external service providers. Absence of clarity in this area will lead to muddled and sub-optimal thinking.

The decision to act: The decision to proceed with the establishment of a family office has significant implications in terms of the expertise required and the methods used for the management of that expertise. The aim of a family office should be to create and maintain quality capabilities and service delivery within a dedicated organisation. This requirement for high levels of expertise applies as much to the family members who are going to be involved in the work of the family office as to the external staff or organisations to be used. Assessing the level of family expertise is clearly going to be a sensitive matter, but is an important one that cannot be ducked.

While a level of trust is a given at the heart of a family office (whether within and between family members, external providers or staff) this has to be supplemented by a risk management and control framework designed to safeguard the family's interests.

Service provision: The final decision on what the family office will provide in terms of scope of services will reflect the family's shared view of what they want, what can reasonably be provided at institution-quality level, and the cost involved. The choice of in-house or external supply will reflect whether the service to be provided is a core one, and the level of proximity and control desired.

Family involvement: The creation of a family office marks a significant investment of the family in the provision of capability for the long-term management of the family's shared interests. This requires the family office to be firmly embedded in the family governance framework and the involvement of family members in the management and oversight of the family office to be clearly defined. All levels of decision making in a family office need to be aligned with the delivery of the family's objectives. The family office also needs to be included in the family's wealth succession plans.

At a more detailed level the following areas that will underpin the design of the family office will need to be discussed:

- staffing;
- systems; and
- policies, processes and procedures.

4.7 Family investment committee

a. Introduction

The unique point and purpose of a family investment committee (or family office board) is to make recommendations to the family council (or, if different, the main body within the family structure that controls ownership) regarding the goal, the objectives and investment strategy that will deliver the family's wealth aspirations. The family investment committee should be charged with delivering on the collective interests of the family.

"Given the complexities families face at this stage of development, careful thought needs to be given to the requirement for, and role to be played by, a family investment committee, as there is likely to be tension between the expectations of the family as it grows and the ability of the family's wealth to keep pace with those expectations."

Strategy discussion by a family investment committee is primarily at the overall family wealth portfolio level, not at the level of the performance of the family enterprise or any other asset or asset class.

While a family investment committee is not always established as part of the governance framework of a family, it is important that its role is represented somewhere within the structure. While some families include the role and functions of an investment committee within the scope of the family council or the family office, doing so can give rise to conflicts of interest that need to be recognised and managed.

The establishment of a family investment committee is most likely to be considered in the following situations:

- where the family invests in a broad range of assets, more than just the family enterprise;
- where there is a broad spread of owners across family branches and generations, rather than where the family is still at the owner/manager stage;
- where the family wants to establish a venture fund to support the development of entrepreneurship within the family; or
- where the family wishes to establish a specific group to assist it in the development, assessment and management of its portfolio of investments, separate from those charged with the running of those investments.

The points discussed below assume that the family has a broad range of assets and is at the multi-branch, multi-generational stage.

Given the complexities families face at this stage of development, careful thought needs to be given to the requirement for, and role to be played by, a family investment committee, as there is likely to be tension between the expectations of the family as it grows and the ability of the family's wealth to keep pace with those expectations. This tension will be further exacerbated if certain assets are seen as being outside the performance criteria required to achieve the target level of performance established by the family.

b. Role

Financial goals and objectives: The starting point for the investment committee is working with the family council on the development of the long-term financial goals and objectives of the family. This is likely to require consideration of the following:

- **Family growth:** As families expand over the generations from the founding family, the rate of growth is considerable. For each family member to maintain their share, the family's wealth will need to grow in line with the rate of growth of the family. (A founding couple are likely to see their family grow to 26 by the time their great-grandchildren are born.)[19] The long-term goal and objectives should recognise this reality.
- **The level of spending/drawing:** The amount of wealth that the family takes out in the form of drawings, dividends or other spending will clearly act as a drag on the growth of the family's wealth. Establishing a policy to govern spending or drawings is likely to enable the family to develop a more sustainable approach to its wealth.
- **Resources available:** The level and nature of, as well as attitudes towards, the resources of the family will influence the family's goal and objectives. Given, also, that much family wealth starts with a family business, thought needs to be given to strategies for the development and/or diversification of the wealth. For example, it would be understandable if the family were to have varying attitudes to the assessment of performance and value of the core family enterprise(s) or other long-held family assets. Equally, consideration needs to be given to which assets are to be included in the family's shared wealth, this being particularly relevant in relation to new business ventures set up by family members.
- **Attitude to risk:** The family's attitude to and tolerance for risk should be articulated as part of the long-term goal and objectives.
- **Liquidity:** The family should establish the level of liquidity they require to hold. This is likely to be to enable the family to meet short-term financing demands such as facilitating the sale/purchase of shares or to make an investment.

Development of investment strategy: With the long-term goal and objectives for the family wealth established, attention can be turned to the investment strategy that will be developed to achieve them. This is likely to involve consideration of the following elements:

- a statement of the goal and objectives for the family's wealth;
- based on the expected return, tolerance for risk and any restrictions placed on any assets or asset classes, the asset classes that can be included in the investment strategy; and
- the asset allocation strategy that appears to optimally deliver the financial return required for the given level of risk. This would typically include an exposure range for each of the asset classes, stating the minimum and maximum exposure levels for that asset class. Few families will start this exercise from scratch – so they will have to take into account the nature and performance of existing assets held when deciding their asset allocation strategy.

Development of investment targets: This is about assisting in the development of the family's investment targets (return, liquidity and risk) for the asset classes within the portfolio. At the individual asset class level the family investment committee will be expected to identify the target levels of return, liquidity and risk that are commensurate with the overall level of return expected by the family. This part of the process would also highlight any restrictions that are to be put in place in respect of any asset class – exposure limits, diversification requirements and so on.

Creation of management and oversight structure: This role involves assisting in the creation of a structure for the management, oversight and monitoring of the asset classes and the family's overall portfolio of investment, and making clear how conflicts of interest are to be managed.

The roles, responsibilities and tasks of those involved should be clearly defined:

- manager selection and monitoring;
- portfolio rebalancing;

- portfolio monitoring;
- portfolio implementation; and
- custody.

c. Membership

The most important issue for consideration in relation to the constitution and membership of the family investment committee is the requirement for sufficient depth and breadth of expertise across the range of investment instruments and asset classes.

Members of the family investment committee should not, however, include any person or persons responsible for the management of the assets falling under the remit of the committee. While such managers will account for their performance to the committee, it is important that they are not members of the committee.

Given that the role of the family investment committee covers the whole of the family's wealth and not just the financial investments of the family, its role could be covered by the ownership council in place within the family governance structure. This might be the family council or a holding company board.

Of critical importance will be the relationship with the family office, which typically covers investment management of financial assets. Here, clarity of role definition, accountability and reporting will all need to be carefully articulated.

The family investment committee may also be charged with responsibility for setting hurdle return rates for new ventures, assessing new ventures and/or funding proposals for new ventures, as well as monitoring their performance.

d. Chair

Any member of the committee may be the chair. It is not unusual for the chair of a family investment committee to be a non-family member, particularly where very significant levels of funds are under management.

e. Meetings and sundries

Meetings are likely to take place quarterly and all papers, reports, etc would be shared back to the family council (or other body) to which the family investment committee reports.

KEY POINTS

The following will all need to be established for the investment committee:

- constitution, including purpose and functions;
- investment framework, including performance expectations and asset allocation;
- membership and expertise, including the extent of external non-family members;
- risk management framework;
- authority limits;
- meeting frequency;
- reporting; and
- agendas.

4.8 Family education committee

a. Introduction

With the successful inter-generational transfer of wealth at the heart of the family vision and governance arrangements, the capability and readiness of the next generations to take on the management and ownership of that wealth is a critical factor. Education (and not just in the formal sense of academic education) of the next generations will be one of the key issues, and this is where the role of an education committee comes in.

There are considerable benefits to an organised approach. It avoids the difficulty of managing individual requests from family members, or an uneven and inconsistent approach, and aside from the benefits that are likely to arise from a more rounded and complete approach there should also be a benefit to having family members undertaking a common programme, with many parts of it undertaken together.

And yet in family enterprise and wealth transition an organised approach to family education is often not thought about or planned for or, where it is, the next generation may be well into their 20s or 30s by the time something more formal is kicked off. Or, something is organised in one branch of the family, but not applied consistently across the whole family.

This often arises because the senior generation, looking to transition the wealth to the next generation, don't think about the issue of next-generation education until they are into their 50s, 60s or 70s. As a result, the opportunity to build the education of the next generation from a very young age, so that the family ethos for the management of their wealth becomes engrained, may be missed.

Some families deliberately choose not to have an open dialogue or discussion of the family's wealth with their children. This can be because the parents' intention is for the family's wealth not to be transitioned to the next generation or because parents do not want their children to become too familiar with, or have expectations of, the family's wealth. This doesn't mean that there is no role for family education – just that in these situations it might be tailored to take the parents' attitudes and objectives into account.

A next-generation education programme will be an undoubted source of feedback and benefit to the senior generation.

b. Role

The scope of the work of a family education committee can cover a very wide range of possible interventions – courses, field visits, job exchanges, junior boards, philanthropy, observing, mentors, coaches, projects/task forces, other board appointments, retreats/team building, membership of other organisations, networking and more.

The objective is for the next generation to be ready for transition within the family or the family business, or in relation to the family wealth. For some next-generation members of the family it might be a combination of all of these; for others, it might be just one.

Being ready is about not only awareness and understanding, but also attitude and values.

Ideally, the acquisition of skills and knowledge will be demonstrated through real, practical involvement in the issues concerned. That way, education can be really and demonstrably embedded.

A positive approach to the education of the next generation may or may not increase the chances of the next generation becoming engaged with the family enterprise; however, it should certainly help to clarify levels of interest, and more importantly prepare family members for a role outside the business. That may still see them involved as owners, but will definitely see them involved as members of the family.

Education of the next generation might cover the following:

- **Understanding the family enterprise:**
  - how family businesses work;
  - the role of family firms;
  - the firm's business strategy;
  - accounting and finance; sales and marketing; manufacturing; operations and administration;
  - ownership and the challenges of continuity and succession;
  - values and culture;
  - board roles and responsibilities; and
  - executive education – MBAs.
- **Developing the next generation:**
  - encouraging entrepreneurship;
  - finance and investing, from starter courses to higher levels of expertise;
  - internships and assignments;
  - working on the front line;
  - assignments in areas such as accounting and finance, sales and marketing, operations and administration;
  - working externally in relevant industries; and
  - leadership coaching and mentoring.
- **Family development:**
  - family history, culture and values;

"Managing small amounts of money, receiving and giving presents, helping out around the home, visiting and helping older relatives, carefully choosing books and stories and family rituals, all allow for the introduction of a young child to money, but also allow the family to relate their values."

- family governance, including family council and assembly activities;
- parenting;
- coping with inherited wealth and dealing with trustees;
- family philanthropy;
- listening and engagement skills;
- personal style; and
- confrontation and conflict management.

Many of the activities listed above will be suited to the next-generation family members at certain points during and in line with their development. While examples of these are shown in Table 7 below, the rationale for undertaking activity through the different stages, particularly the early years, is set out in the following sections.

Early years: The early years – up to the age of 11 – are primarily centred on the family and home. Matters pertaining to wealth or money are likely to involve things like sharing and helping; understanding limits and unmet desires; developing early passions, cares and attachments; and perhaps beginning to introduce a sense of purpose.

Managing small amounts of money, receiving and giving presents, helping out around the home, visiting and helping older relatives, carefully choosing books and stories and family rituals, all allow for the introduction of a young child to money, but also allow the family to relate their values.

Children of this age will have little sense of the family enterprise or where the family wealth comes from. Parents of children in this age bracket are likely to be in their 30s and early 40s, building their own careers and wealth, often with large outgoings associated with bringing up young children and establishing the family home. The management of money might need to balance income with large outgoings. Time can be precious, meaning focus on the education of young children about the value of money might not be at the forefront of parental thinking.

The importance of the early years cannot be overestimated, as research indicates that the early years play a big role in determining whether a child will be a spender or a saver.

Early teens: The early teens see children start to have to deal with external influences, whether these arise through their formal education, school trips, the internet or, increasingly over more recent times, social media. Children, particularly if attending private school, will begin to see how their friends and peers behave in relation to money, all out of the gaze and control of their parents.

Parents of children at this stage can sometimes exhibit a tendency to believe that their children are still very young, and as a result can underestimate how their parental behaviours are registered by their children. Parents are now going to be into their mid-40s and early 50s, meaning there may well be more availability of wealth, but very probably considerable work pressures as many parents will be entering the peak period of their careers. At this stage, wealth can be deployed to keep life simple and manageable, and is likely to see high levels of discretionary expenditure. Perhaps not consciously, but certainly subconsciously, these experiences and pressures are likely to form norms for family relationships, and further influence the next generation's attitude to wealth and money.

For some families, early retirement or reduced working may be an option. While this can afford the opportunity for parents to spend more time with their children, often the wealth that has enabled retirement begins to finance a more relaxed and pleasurable lifestyle. As this happens, in some families the children can lose touch with the drive, passion and energy that enabled their parents to create success, the fruits of which they are now enjoying.

As relationships change, communication levels can change too. Constancy and security are really important. The aim is for the next generation to have sufficient confidence to define themselves by their actions rather than money, and for the parents to validate this with wider family and friends and not just with their children.

Early adulthood: This phase sees the young person growing into adulthood, backed by recognition through the legal system in many countries.

Grappling with school exams, beginning to think about tertiary education and possibly even career choices – this is a vital stage. But it's also the stage where many young adults will move away from the family home, and live independently for the first time. Budgeting, personal accountability and dealing with the consequences of actions all have to be confronted. For young adults from wealthy or prominent families, they may also have to deal with name recognition, away from the relative safety of the community at their school or college. Readiness and coping in an independent setting are key.

Parents' relationships with their children at this stage can be complex. There are many positives to come from the young adult stage, for example enjoyment of a wider range of more interesting and exciting activities where parent and child are beginning to be more equal. Parents have to balance the challenge and emotion of letting their child go with providing support and backup for them as they adapt to their new-found independence and freedom – it can appear quite thankless!

Yet wealth and money may find parents providing too much, such that a sense of responsibility, particularly financial, in the young adult may be lost. In some families, particularly where the parents who have generated the wealth came from modest backgrounds themselves, this can be the result of an over-compensation with their children.

Into adulthood: As the next-generation family members move into full adulthood, they are likely to experience the challenges of balancing a number of different desires and motivations: personal and professional growth, a desire to express themselves creatively, the need to express and experience their independence, and wanting a sense of achievement and progress. All of these can be challenging when set within the confines of a family enterprise or family wealth.

As this sense of growth and creativity is expressed and supported, hopefully the foundations established by the earlier stages will have established the right values in the next generation and provided a variety of links and connections within the family and the family enterprise. It is a key reason for establishing a family education framework across the three pillars outlined in Table 7 below.

It can be helpful for the family education committee to plot out the phases and changes expected within the next generation over time, as shown in the table. The committee will also need to assess the level of expenditure that the family will commit to the education programme, including provision for school and university fees.

c. Membership

Membership of the family education committee will typically comprise one or more members of the family council and of the wider family – both those working in the family business and those not. Bringing in representatives of the different generations will assist in engaging the next generations, giving them a say in the development of the family education curriculum.

d. Chair

While not crucial, it will be helpful for the chair to be a member of the family council.

e. Meetings and sundries

Terms of reference for the family education committee should be developed. Providing it with a more formal footing will enable its plans to be embedded within the work of the family council.

The committee might be expected to meet once or twice a year to review the education curriculum and the progress of different family members. It will submit progress reports and updated plans to the family council, as well as seek budget support for any initiatives.

Table 7. Stages of next-generation development

Age	Understanding the family enterprise	Next-gen development	Family development
<11	Becoming aware of the family enterprise, and its longevity, through occasional visits with parents and grandparents	Managing allowances and the concepts of spending/saving/giving Developing proportionate sense of value of money	Building family relationships across generations and branches Beginning to understand family history Beginning to feel a sense of key family values Storytelling Being involved in small-scale family philanthropy projects
11–16	Starting to understand the various family members in the business and their roles Understanding the history of the business and some of its key decisions and developments Experiencing summer internships and junior boards in latter part of phase Understanding the family employment policy Having conversations about the family enterprise and talking openly with parents about their roles	Carrying out basic budgeting Earning; understanding pay, taxes, savings goals and interest Joining school trips and volunteering Receiving support for final exam choices and university selection Having early discussions about career paths	Moving from an informal approach to family relationships to involvement with the family assembly and awareness of the family council and other family governance assemblies/bodies Taking part in activities to reinforce family values and validate next-gen contribution Being part of kitchen table family philanthropy and family project trips Having purposeful conversations about family interactions and gaining feedback on engagements

continued on next page

Age	Understanding the family enterprise	Next-gen development	Family development
17–22	Role-shadowing Taking summer employment (in and outside the family business) Meeting senior management and wider staff Undertaking *ad hoc* research projects for the family business, eg, on new product development, competitor research and customer research Being exposed to new ventures and projects Taking junior board positions and observing full boards Understanding ownership within the family enterprise	Undertaking holiday planning and expenditure Having access to family education grants Managing university spending, loans and rent Understanding interest rates and dividends Volunteering for community projects Beginning to understand financial reports and reports on investment management Receiving seed funding for business ideas	Attending family assembly meetings Being exposed to the wider family governance framework and key policies Beginning to engage on family council matters Taking junior board or observer role in family philanthropic entity Starting to develop own philanthropy funding plan Starting to lead creation of family assembly activity
>22	Taking employee roles if working in the business Charting a career path to move through the different areas of the business Demonstrating full understanding of the family business (may well have an ownership stake)	Enjoying leadership development Taking part in coaching and mentoring Taking roles in external companies Completing MBA or executive education programmes	Actively engaging in and possibly leading certain aspects of the family governance

KEY POINTS

There are perhaps three key points that underpin the creation of a family education committee and that come before the detailed considerations of scope and activities set out above. The questions below are predicated on the fact that the overall family wealth philosophy, vision and values have already been agreed and set out.

Does the senior generation have a clear philosophy for the involvement of the next generation in the family enterprise or wealth? This should ideally drive and capture the family's wishes as to the timing and extent of the communication and education process for the next generation.

Families can have quite significant differences in approach to this topic:

- Some prefer to delay communication with the next generation until they are older or judged old enough to be able to cope with the pressure the wealth will bring.
- Others prefer to take the approach of demonstrating the values that sit behind their wealth, rather than talking about the wealth itself.
- Another approach favoured by some families is to be very open from the start.
- And of course some families believe that the next generation should generate their own fortunes and not have access to the wealth that they have generated.
- For families with a family business, some believe that the next generation should go off and gain external experience before coming into the family business.
- Others believe that the next generation should start at the bottom and work their way up, starting in their teens with holiday work and intern roles.

Each of these approaches has merits and drawbacks. However, depending on the response to the main question, the family should be able to build a framework for communication between family members and the generations.

As the next generation move into their teen years, this issue might link to the family employment policy and, to the extent that the family is active in philanthropy, to the family philanthropy committee.

What is the focus of the family education committee? This takes the family's philosophy and turns it into a plan of action. At a high level is it about the family business, financial education, and/or careers. The identified focus will begin to detail the issues to be covered as well as the phasing of education.

Who pays? Who has access? Who makes provision? Finally, the family will need to decide where the cost of the education will be borne, which members of the family have access to it and who the family will work with in the provision of the education. Certain elements of education provision may be quite costly, but equally may not be appropriate for every member of the family at a certain age/life stage. This question becomes important as families grow in terms of the breadth and number of generations. It can even become an issue of family fairness.

4.9 Family philanthropy committee

a. Introduction

This section is about the role philanthropy can play in family governance. While it covers the motivation, structure and approach for philanthropy, it is not about the merits or otherwise of philanthropy *per se*, nor do we focus on a particular or tight definition of philanthropy. It could, for example, cover social investment or impact investing in addition to what we might think of as philanthropy.

Philanthropy, in the context of family governance, offers a family a range of opportunities to support the achievement of its vision as well as to support the management and transition of the family's wealth.

In particular, it can:

- engage a wider and different cross-section of the family than

those involved in the family business or the management of the family wealth;
- provide the family with a new opportunity to work together that can be non-hierarchical and not focused on the family's wealth, but on beneficiaries and causes outside the family;
- provide the younger generations with an opportunity to see and influence the way the family works; and
- provide a training and development opportunity for the next generation of the family, in areas such as the family's values, investments, governance, working together and decision making.

Over time, a family's approach to philanthropy can also help to provide a historical context for, and link to, the family's values, and can help to develop a real sense of the value of money in the younger generation.

The rise of philanthropy alongside newly generated wealth is seeing a number of emerging trends. Younger and next-generation philanthropists are more socially aware, global in outlook and social media savvy. This can be seen as a challenge to more traditional forms of family philanthropy, or it can be embraced as an opportunity for the next generation to bring a new dimension to the family community, whether in the form of social enterprise, social investment or impact investing. It can also bring an opportunity for the senior generations to see the way the younger ones engage with new, social media channels as well as new opportunities for the family and its wealth.

b. Role

Philanthropy within families can come in many guises. It can be organised in a number of ways:
- informally (what we might term kitchen table philanthropy);
- as a family fund or foundation; or
- as family business philanthropy.

Family philanthropy can also be tied to a family's religious beliefs through, for example, *zakat*, *tzedakah* or tithing. And a number of entities, informal through to legal, exist to support a family's approach.

Kitchen table philanthropy: This, as the term implies, is a very informal approach to philanthropy. Discussions regarding the philanthropic actions a family will take are proposed, discussed and agreed in an informal setting with a flexible approach to the family members taking part and the causes or charities that the family will support. Typically, family members are asked to bring suggestions for support; these are then discussed by those taking part and decisions taken as to which organisations to support. Ordinarily, the level of funds available for each session and cause to be supported are relatively modest.

Family fund or foundation: This is a formal approach to philanthropy where a legal entity is set up to carry out the philanthropic activities. This has a number of consequences that mean the approach can no longer be informal:

- A clear purpose or objects clause is set down in the legal documentation.
- Individuals are formally appointed with legal responsibility for operating the philanthropic structure.
- Clear financial arrangements will be established. Aside from banking arrangements, there may also be a need to maintain financial records and have these subjected to external review.
- In some jurisdictions, there is a requirement for the entity to be registered with a regulatory body that may or may not make the details of the income and spend of the entity, and those with responsibility for it, available publicly.

Family business philanthropy: This approach sees the funding organised through the family company, with the accountability for the philanthropy fitting in with the corporate structure and control mechanisms. The approach needs to take careful account of the laws and regulation of the country in which the company is based, as there are restrictions regarding benefit, and the taxation treatment of any charitable gifts varies.

Internationally, there are a range of legal entities for philanthropy. For ease of reference we have provided a generalised description of the two main types of entity that exist (recognising that they may not both exist in all jurisdictions):

Donor-advised fund: This is a charitable fund established under the legal ownership of another, usually charitable, body that holds philanthropic funds for the family that are invested and distributed at the family's behest. Such funds do not require separate legal or regulatory registration and the administration and record keeping is greatly simplified.

Charitable foundation:[20] This is a separate legal entity formed specifically with (usually exclusively) charitable objectives. The entity has a separate legal identity, but this requires a governance and management framework to be established, often with legal, regulatory and financial disclosure and filing requirements. As such, it will require family members to take on the obligations of the formal roles put in place for the management of the entity.

Regardless of the form used, it is important that the family establishes a strategic approach to its philanthropic activity. Addressing the three key questions below should enable a family to do this:

Why are we doing this? Answering the Why question first is really important as it allows an aligned and strategic approach to the family's philanthropy to emerge. The temptation is to get into the What and How before the Why is settled, but it's important that this is resisted.

The Why question is about getting in touch with the family's motivation for wanting to be a philanthropic family. It inevitably touches on what the family wants to achieve, but it's more about understanding the reasons for doing philanthropy than answering what the family wants to achieve – that's answered by the What question.

Experience tells us that the motivations can be quite varied. Understanding and articulating the motivation allows for clear goals and objectives and, consequently, an approach that provides a better chance of them being achieved. The table below sets out three common motivations and how they can steer the approach.

Table 8. Philanthropy – motivation and approach

Motivation	Approach
High-impact philanthropy	Often the domain of the very entrepreneurial or investment-focused philanthropist, this form of philanthropy focuses on high-impact actions and outcomes. Usually supported by a hands-on approach, the philanthropist will be looking to build scale, at pace, to deliver strong impact.
Family education	Where philanthropy is used to develop family education, the involvement of the next generation will be high, whether through formal board roles or a next-generation philanthropy committee. While the philanthropic approach should be no less strategic, the main focus will be on the involvement and development of the next generation, meaning that their philanthropic ideas and actions are likely to gain prominence.
Use for surplus wealth	Once a family has acquired surplus wealth, there are only two areas in which that wealth can be deployed – family or philanthropy. Many wealthy families prefer that their surplus wealth is given away rather than given to the next generation. A giving pledge is a good example of the deployment of surplus wealth for philanthropic purposes. The approach taken is likely to be closely aligned with the areas of personal passion and interest of the wealth generator.

It should flow naturally from asking and answering the Why question, but it's really important to check that there's a clear and explicit link between goals and objectives of philanthropy, on the one hand, and the family's values on the other.

What are we going to do? This question is not just about the cause focus of the family; it's also about the impact that's going to be created.

It is typical within families that the interests of the family members vary. A decision needs to be taken as to whether the family's approach will allow for this breadth of interest or whether it will focus on a narrower set of objectives. Determining which voices within the family are heard is likely to influence the level of engagement from across the family. Conversely a broader range of activities might lessen the scale of the impact that can be created.

In answering the What question the scale of the financial commitment should also be set out. This should include whether the funding will be on a flow-through or endowed basis.

How are we going to do this? The How takes into account the earlier points about the form in which the philanthropy is to be conducted, but also considers how the philanthropic actions are going to be delivered. The most usual form is to provide grant funds to another organisation to deliver the philanthropic actions.

Depending on the scale of the family's philanthropy, decisions will need to be taken on the staffing required to support the philanthropic programme. This might entail hiring non-family staff or having dedicated family members working on the philanthropy programme.

The How also entails thinking through the decision-making processes and procedures for the family's philanthropy and will, at a high level, include the following:

- beneficiary identification and selection;
- the grant-making process, including the form of agreements to be used;
- due diligence; and
- reporting and monitoring.

c. Membership

The presence of a philanthropy committee (or equivalent) within the family governance framework provides an opportunity to bring together a diverse group from the family, not only across the generations and multiple family branches, but also family members not so closely involved in the management of the family business or family wealth.

While the legal nature of the structure used might require a more formal recognition of the membership role, such recognition can equally apply in a more informal approach, where it can be helpful to establish rules for the selection, terms and stepping down of the members of the controlling body. Some families also introduce a next-generation group to work informally alongside the main controlling group, enabling the family to bring on the younger generation of family members. This can allow family members below the age of 18 to start to become involved in the systems of management and governance of the family wealth.

Where a more formal approach is taken that requires legally appointed representatives, additional attention should be paid to the way the membership of the controlling body is organised and managed, in both the controlling documents of the philanthropic structure and in the way that appointments are managed.

As some families will introduce independent, non-family members to the controlling body, care needs to be taken in a number of areas, for example:

- the balance of family and non-family members on the controlling body, and whether a majority of bloodline family members will be in the majority;
- how appointments to the controlling body are made, how the terms of office are governed, recorded and managed, and whether there are grounds for dismissal of members of the controlling body; and
- any requirement for long-stop arrangements that keep the philanthropic structure within the governance control of family members.

d. Chair

The chair role for the family's philanthropy offers the opportunity for the individual selected to really develop the opportunities it affords, whether with regard to the social impact of the philanthropic activity or the developmental opportunities for the family members involved.

Terms of office for key roles in philanthropic structures, and not just for the chair, are increasingly the norm, with three-year terms the standard. In addition, there is often a three-term limit, meaning a maximum overall term as chair of nine years. As well as being a sign of good governance, this allows for the renewal of the family's philanthropic purpose and objectives.

The appointment and review process for the chair role would normally be handled by the family council.

e. Meetings and sundries

The approach to the working of the family's philanthropy will depend on the structure selected. If a legal entity approach is adopted that requires registration, there will be a prescribed form of governance that will need to be adopted. For informal approaches the family can decide how to structure things.

Family philanthropy is normally structured around six-monthly meetings at which grant decisions are made, and programmes and projects that have been funded are monitored.

KEY POINTS

Some of the key issues for the family's philanthropy strategy that will need to be agreed are as follows:

Scope of the philanthropy: There can be a tendency in family philanthropy for a wide number of project or programme possibilities to be put forward for funding, whether by individual family members, a family branch or a group from a particular generation. This can flow from a well-meaning desire to please the members of the family and to encourage involvement, but there is a risk that this can erode the strategic focus and the impact that can be achieved. It's important, therefore, for a proper process of consultation and strategic development to take place to determine the areas of work and support. Rather than supporting a wide range of ideas that appeal to individuals, a family should be seeking to identify an area that drives consensus and is closely aligned to the family purpose and values, in a field of work that can potentially be sustained.

Funding: Assuming that a strategic approach is being taken to the family's philanthropy, then the level of funding should be sufficient to enable the family to pursue its objectives. There are two primary funding routes:

- an endowment basis, where the return or yield on the investment is spent; or
- a 'flow-through' basis, which basically sees annual donations made to the philanthropic entity to match expected outflows over that timeframe.

The former has the benefit of letting the wider family work through the dynamics of investing capital to produce a return to fund the philanthropic aspirations, while the latter approach provides a more efficient allocation of capital, without tying it up in a form in which it can't be used for other purposes.

Resourcing: Aside from the funding, consideration also needs to be given to the level of resourcing required to manage the family's philanthropy. Does the family have the requisite level of internal expertise, or is external management support required? This covers not just the philanthropic activities but also all of the administration activities such as book-keeping, meeting support and documentation.

'Youngest child' syndrome: There can be a tendency within some families for the philanthropy to become the domain of the youngest child. The term can be seen as a euphemism for an activity that is seen as less important than running the family business or the family investment activities.

This can be for a number of different reasons, but it is an issue to be aware of. Of prime importance is that the reason for the family being involved in philanthropy is clearly articulated, and the activity designed and supported in line with the family's overall and philanthropic objectives.

Mode of operation: Social impact can be achieved through routes other than just philanthropy (eg, social investment or impact investing) so it's important that the merits and implications of the different routes are thought through.

4.10 Family arbitration committee

a. Introduction

A family arbitration committee is established within a family governance framework in recognition of the fact that the affairs of families are unlikely to run entirely smoothly all of the time. Discussion of an arbitration committee can feel strange when times are good, but setting up a family governance structure is all about creating a framework to deal with difficulties, should they arise in the future. So discussing family arbitration arrangements shouldn't be as surprising as it often feels for families.

The simple fact is that nearly all families will, at some time or other, experience disputes, differences of opinion, friction, incongruity and/or divided loyalties. In many cases little or no harm is done and very often relationships are smoothed over quite quickly, albeit family members may resort to classic reactions such as ignoring each other, raising voices or trying to deflect the issue by involving others, before moving on and getting over things.

In a smaller number of cases things get serious, and this can be when conflict arises and a more serious way of tackling the conflict is required. While there are several different non-legal approaches to family dispute resolution and these approaches may be employed by the family first, arbitration as a method tends to be quick, cost effective and definitive. It is also a private process that keeps the family dispute and its resolution out of the glare of publicity.

Family conflict and thus the need for a family arbitration committee is more likely to be relevant in a multi-branch, multi-generational family involving a more complex family/family business dynamic.

The causes of family disputes are relatively simple to outline but can be hard to fully understand, the more so when positions become hardened or the source of a dispute becomes clouded in a wider family falling-out. They include the following:

- Treatment opportunity, reward or responsibility differs between family members.
- Different family members play different roles.
- Expectations of family members differ.
- There is a breach of trust or confidence, or a failure to uphold standards.

Add to this the dynamics of a family business – the many roles that can be played (sometimes multiple roles for one person); levels of responsibility; access to information; involvement in decision making that affects family members; and the multiple sources of income and wealth, not always evenly distributed, involved – and it's little wonder that the opportunity for family disputes increases.

Many of these issues arise in families without them becoming harmful. Issues tend only to become harmful when they are not discussed and/or addressed and are left to fester – positions then harden. At this point the degree of difference becomes deep-seated, almost a grievance, from which a strong sense of unfairness arises, where self-responsibility might be abandoned, where fault is attributed to someone else and for which redress is sought. It matters not whether the underlying cause was real or perceived.

Examples might include:

- family members perceiving that the family or family firm hasn't fulfilled its obligations to them;
- siblings believing that they are the subject of unequal or inconsistent treatment – whether that be opportunity, reward or even involvement;

- in-laws believing another family member is receiving preferential treatment; or
- power or decision making appearing to be concentrated within a certain group of family members to the exclusion of others, without proper explanation.

Families and family businesses are highly individual entities, with varying degrees of complexity. Issues that one family can cope with may easily be the source of major divergence or disagreement in another. Dealing with them requires experience and a delicate touch.

There is a difference between the occasional, albeit strong, disagreement and an issue that comes before a family arbitration committee reflecting a deep-rooted problem that has been allowed to grow, and that should have been dealt with earlier. The job of a family arbitration committee shouldn't be seen only as dealing with problems once they arise – it should extend to the general mood and atmosphere in a family such as to avoid the problems coming up at all. It should aim to recognise problems as soon as they start to become issues, and to seek, informally, to prevent them escalating into full-blown family conflicts.

b. Role

It is important to determine the scope of the arbitration committee's remit. Normally it includes matters that arise within the family, but not those that arise in the family business. The latter can and should be dealt with by the managers or board of the family business. Typically, the arbitration committee will deal with issues that concern breaches of the family governance framework or the family code of conduct.

The family arbitration committee seeks to resolve issues within the bounds of the family and to prevent them becoming issues where, in a worst case scenario, external legal redress might be sought. To this end it is important that all family members covered by the family governance framework sign up to the governance framework's approach to the manner in which family conflict is managed, and in particular that they recognise the role and powers of the arbitration committee in the context of the family's best interests.

"The committee is focused on resolving difficulties and ensuring fairness. To balance the family nature of things, it is helpful to have an independent, non-family committee member, experienced in family dispute resolution in general and arbitration in particular."

This is significant, as the role of the arbitration committee is to see disputes settled through an arbitration process that makes a decision that is binding on the parties. It is not a consensual or collaborative process. The party against whom the committee makes the award won't have the ability to appeal the decision, assuming it has been validly made. They may, however, attempt to appeal against the process – hence the need for the committee to have robust procedures in place.

Arbitration might be seen as the final stage of a dispute resolution process that includes earlier stages seeking a more collaborative or consensual approach.

c. Membership

The committee is focused on resolving difficulties and ensuring fairness. To balance the family nature of things, it is helpful to have an independent, non-family committee member, experienced in family dispute resolution in general and arbitration in particular.

Given that the committee is established to deal with difficulties arising in the family, it is important that it is clearly constituted and run in order to minimise challenges to its legitimacy. There should be a clear mechanism for establishing its membership; clear terms of reference for members; and provision for recusal, either permanently or temporarily, where a member finds him or herself with a conflict of interest in respect of a family member either bringing a matter to the committee or responding to enquiries by the committee.

With the committee focused on dealing with family matters and not on matters arising in relation to the family business, members of the committee should be drawn from the family-orientated part of the governance structure.

A committee membership of three should suffice, made up as follows:

- chair of the family council, as the chair is, in effect, head of the family;
- a further family member elected by the family council, but not necessarily someone who is a member of the family council; and

- an independent expert in arbitration proceedings – a non-family individual, appointed by the family council, bringing an appropriate degree of rigour and independence to the committee and its work.

d. Chair

Given the membership basis discussed above, it would make sense for the family council chair to chair the arbitration committee.

e. Meetings and sundries

Once established, the committee is more likely to meet on a case-by-case basis rather than there being regular meetings.

The committee will need to establish the processes by which it conducts itself.

The committee will need a clear voting mechanism, and will need to establish criteria for decision making (for example, what's best for the family) as well as determining what awards will be made.

KEY POINTS

The following points are likely to need discussion in relation to the family arbitration committee:

Sources of conflict: As part of the creation or review of a family governance framework or family constitution, the family should consider potential sources of conflict, specifically within the family. One of the key reasons for family-wide involvement in the creation and review of family governance is to help all family members believe they are part of the creation process and have had their say in the framework by which the family will operate. That said, families often have deeply rooted ways of doing things or traditions that may seem odd or not be fully understood by outsiders (eg, spouses) coming into the family.

Perhaps the largest number of disputes within families are linked to issues to do with money or control. While money issues are relatively straightforward to assess, control issues, particularly as they are often to do with emotional control, can be hidden or tend not to be spoken about. Even where they are known about and acknowledged, doing something about them can be extremely difficult. Families that are set up with an uneven balance within the areas of money or control will in all likelihood be more susceptible to disputes.

The other area that can cause difficulty is behaviour that threatens the reputation of the family. In this respect, families may need to think about bespoke approaches to conflict and to family myths about conflict, perhaps by undertaking a family culture assessment to help bring into the open the potentially unhelpful things that members do without necessarily understanding how or why.

Application of provisions: Consideration should be given to the number of family members to whom conflict resolution provisions apply. While it makes sense for them to apply to family members with some form of ownership stake in the family business, and possibly to those to whom financial support is provided (ie, beneficiaries), it is may be less important for wider family members to be covered. That said, if families are concerned about reputational issues then it may make sense for the provisions to have wider application.

Minimising conflict: Developing the idea that prevention is better than cure, thought could be given to what can or should be done, on an ongoing basis, proactively within the family governance framework, to minimise the chances of disputes arising. The family governance framework has many elements that can be used to assist the family in this regard, whether they be for communication, education or induction of new family members, all of which can be used to minimise the chances of a dispute.

Other means of resolution: In the event that a dispute does arise there is no need for arbitration to be the only means of settling it. Other means include adjudication, mediation, negotiation, conciliation, intervention, interposition or peace-making. It may make sense for families to try one or more of these approaches before setting in train an arbitration process.

4.11 Family remuneration committee

a. Introduction

A family remuneration committee is concerned with the establishment and maintenance of a policy regarding the fixing and reviewing of remuneration of family members employed within the family business and wealth structures.

The committee primarily concerns itself with employment remuneration as opposed to remuneration issues relating to ownership of the company. This is an important distinction. The operation of the remuneration policy should be underpinned by an approach to remuneration that supports the sustainability of the company or structure in the market(s) within which it operates and provides the level of return required by the owners. This will require the committee to use suitable external information and create appropriate comparators and benchmarks.

All aspects of remuneration of family members are potentially a source of difficulty, disagreement or even conflict within the family (primarily between those working for the family and those not), and may even be the source of difficulties with non-family employees. A clear approach and clear processes for family remuneration can reduce the likelihood of these difficulties arising.

It's worth noting that the need for a formally established family remuneration committee is likely to increase as the number of family members working for the family increases.

b. Role

The family remuneration committee is established by and should report to the family council, as the body that represents the owners of the business. A clear determination should be made as to the range and level of powers either delegated to the remuneration committee or retained by the family council.

The role of the family remuneration committee might cover all aspects of remuneration, incentives and other benefits of family members working for the family. These might include pensions, company cars, the setting of performance objectives and performance appraisal, as well as policy and process regarding expenses.

It is important that adequate consideration is given to the purpose and scope of the committee's activities, as the role of the committee, where it covers wider remuneration issues for the family business, will touch upon remuneration policy and practices in respect of non-family members employed in the family business.

Where a remuneration committee is established, care should be taken with regard to the relationship with the board of directors of the family business. Remuneration issues in a company would normally be within the remit of the board, so if certain remuneration issues are reserved for the family remuneration committee, any resulting friction between the two bodies could generate difficulties in the functioning of the family business.

The terms of reference for the family remuneration committee should be signed off by the family council and the board of directors of the family business.

It is possible to combine the committee with the functions of a family employment committee. In the absence of a formally established remuneration committee, its functions could be carried out by the family council or a sub-group of the family council.

c. Membership

A membership of three should ordinarily be sufficient for a family remuneration committee, comprising two family members and one independent member, who would bring an appropriate level of skill and experience in the area of remuneration.

The experience of the independent member of the committee is important as this individual should bring, on the one hand, the skills and experience to establish a robust approach to the issue of remuneration based on sound practices, and on the other an independence of viewpoint that should be reassuring to the key stakeholders in the decisions reached by the committee – family members employed in the business, family members not employed in the business, and non-family members working in the business.

Of the two family members, there is some benefit in having one who does not work in the family business. This should balance the perspectives of family members who both do and do not work in the business, and should allow the views of both parties to be adequately represented on the issue of pay and rewards of those family members who do work in the family business.

The two family members of the remuneration committee should be elected by the family council, with the independent member being nominated by the family council.

d. Chair

The family council will elect the chair from the two family members. This is an important role given the sensitivities surrounding pay for family members working in the family business.

e. Meetings and sundries

Proceedings of the committee and minutes of its meetings should be shared with the family council, and possibly the board. Clearly, from time to time sensitive matters will be discussed, and the chair will need to agree with the respective chairs of the family council and family business board how these should be handled.

A minimum of two meetings per year are likely to be required – one to consider and set performance aspirations, the other to review proposed pay awards. One of the meetings should also consider market trends and the impact on benchmarks, and review the policy annually.

KEY POINTS

The following points are likely to need discussion in relation to the family remuneration committee:

Conflicts of interest: The area of remuneration is likely to bring a number of competing interests into play, and may even involve some conflicts of interest. Issues relating to the remuneration of family members working in the business are likely to be of interest to a number of different parties involved in the governance of the family and the family business, and it is important to ensure that this is taken into account in the committee's work.

In addition to remuneration, lines of accountability, decision making, reporting and communication should all be considered.

Role and function: A remuneration committee is more likely to be required within a family governance structure in the following circumstances:

- when there are a reasonable number of family members working for the family or seeking to work for the family;
- where family members from different generations and family branches are working for the family;
- where family members working for the family occupy a range of different positions at different levels;
- where spouses or other non-bloodline relatives of family members are working for the family;
- where there are non-family owners of the family business; and
- where the family business is of sufficient size/scale to require remuneration to be benchmarked to the external market.

A choice exists as to whether to establish the remuneration committee formally as a separate body within the family governance structure or allow its functions to be undertaken on a less formal basis, within the auspices of the family council, either as a business item or possibly as a working group of the family council.

Remuneration philosophy: Setting a clear remuneration philosophy is one of the key tasks for a remuneration committee, whatever its form within the family governance structure. This is important, as the levels and scope of reward can be a source of difficulty and even conflict between those family members working in the family business, family owners who do not work in the business, wider family members neither working in the business nor owners, and non-family members working in the family business.

In this regard, transparency as to the issues considered by the family remuneration committee will be important.

Remuneration philosophy is likely to address the following questions:

- What is the point and purpose of remuneration within the wider family governance framework, that is, is it specifically a reward for the role undertaken, the responsibilities attached to the role and the performance delivered, or does remuneration serve some wider purpose? For example, it is not unusual for a 'family premium' to be included in the remuneration of certain key individuals within the family. The family premium might include recompense for the opportunities foregone outside the family business, a desire to promote loyalty and continuity, or even limitations placed on other activities that a family member can undertake.
- What overall level of remuneration can the family business bear? The level and breadth of remuneration and reward included in the remuneration policy will bear upon the results of the family business, and ultimately impact the returns available to the owners.
- What elements of reward are to be included in the remuneration policy? Salary, bonuses, long-term incentives, pensions and other benefits can all be included. For benefits, the issue of who bears the tax also needs to be considered.
- What are the appropriate benchmarks for the remuneration offered? Consideration here needs to include comparator industries, geographical areas, company size, role definitions and levels, as well as a determination of how competitive the reward packages should be.

- What employment terms and conditions, restrictions on activity and other employment terms should be considered?

Independent members: Given the range of interests in the area of remuneration, the use of an independent expert provides an opportunity to bring external and neutral perspective; however, bringing in an external person to such a sensitive area can present difficulties.

4.12 Family employment committee

a. Introduction

The issues that fall within the remit of a family employment committee are some of the most critical for a family in that they concern the development of future leaders and, ultimately, the continuity of the family business and wealth.

Clarity of expectations around family employment and its rewards is likely to assist the family in preparing for dealing with future issues regarding fairness of treatment of family members or setting and managing expectations of family members for the future, and in avoiding or diffusing future disagreement or even conflict.

Equally important is the creation of guidance for family members who choose not to come into family employment. Will it be possible for them to join later? What if they choose to pursue entrepreneurial business ideas of their own?

Experience suggests that action around the creation of a family employment strategy and supporting policies is not something that happens in the early stages of the development of a multi-generational family business and wealth. During the transition between G1 and G2 the issues are more often associated with encouraging the next generation to become involved with the family business and wealth. Next-generation family members (and sometimes spouses too) may become employed by the family without full regard to what it means for the future, thus making retro-fitting family employment practices onto a family business or wealth structure more difficult.

While strategic discussion of family employment issues should take place at the family council (or equivalent), the implementation of the resulting direction will fall to the body charged with managing family employment issues.

A family employment committee is concerned with far more than just setting policy and managing processes relating to the employment of family members. It might be responsible for implementing approaches that encourage and support future family members to become involved with the business and wealth; how their careers are developed and managed; how spouses are treated; and how family members who choose not to work for the family develop their careers.

The creation of clear policy and practice is not just important for the family employees; it is equally, if not more, important for non-family employees. This distinction becomes even more evident when there are non-family board directors and managers charged with making appointment decisions regarding family members. They will be just as concerned that there is a clear framework for managing employment and personnel decisions, thereby minimising the possibility of charges of (let alone actual) nepotism or favouritism.

The requirement for a family employment framework is likely to grow in the following scenarios:

- where the family business and wealth is substantial;
- where the family is both large and multi-generational; and
- where the business and wealth involves a mix of family and non-family members in critical roles.

b. Role

The family employment committee is established by, and should report to, the family council as the body that represents the owners of the business. Like a number of other committees, it is possible for the role of the employment committee to be retained by the family council or merged into another committee's role, possibly the remuneration committee. Either way, what is important is that where a family intends to employ family members there is a clear understanding, preferably recorded in written terms, regarding how this is managed.

As with the family remuneration committee, care should be taken to establish a clear relationship with the board of directors of the family business or other structures. Employment decisions, as opposed to policy, within a company would normally be within the remit of the board and senior management, guided by the employment policy. If, however, decisions are reserved for the family employment committee or family council, there arises the possibility of friction between the two bodies and difficulties in the functioning of the family business.

The terms of reference for the committee should be signed off by the family council and the board of directors of the family business.

c. Family employment policy

The family employment policy should make clear a number of critical points, and then provide a framework that sets out the employment practices that the directors and management of the family business will operate.

Overarching employment principles: These principles are important as they lie at the heart of developing continuity of family involvement in the family wealth. It often follows that they are likely to provide strong encouragement to the next generation to become involved, but care must be taken to ensure that the family does not compromise on the quality of the people its employs. As such, the principles are likely to provide clarity regarding the following:

- **Basis of roles:** This refers to the basis upon which employment roles in the family are encouraged and facilitated. For example, the principles would be likely to establish the extent of the encouragement provided to younger members of the family to enable them to become familiar with the operations and activities of the family business and wealth. This might include attending and observing meetings or activities within the family business, summer jobs, work experience, internships, or part-time employment. Criteria for these different positions would be expected to be set out.
- **Criteria for employment:** While it is almost a given that families will encourage the next generation to be involved and employed

"For those family members identified as having potential to move to senior levels, it is likely that they will be expected to work and hold positions right across the business and wealth, often being moved into positions without the level of experience and qualifications that external hires would be expected to demonstrate."

in the management of the family business and wealth, it is unlikely that roles will be guaranteed, that is, that they will be a birthright. It follows that certain criteria are likely to be set down. These might include the following requirements:

- that all positions held by family have a business justification;
- that all appointees have the experience and qualifications expected of non-family applicants for a given role; or
- that all positions are assessed against external applicants, with an 'at least as good as' proviso for a family member to be appointed.

For more senior roles, or where there is a specialist nature to a role, there may be a requirement for a certain amount of external experience or a certain level of educational qualification.

- **Terms and conditions for employment:** It will be expected that the policy establish terms, conditions and compensation on the same basis as for non-family employees, and that family employees perform against similar performance standards and uphold similar behaviours and values. Importantly, compensation for employment should be separate from the benefits of ownership.
- **Career development:** Career plans for family members are likely to be different from the majority of non-family employees. For those family members identified as having potential to move to senior levels, it is likely that they will be expected to work and hold positions right across the business and wealth, often being moved into positions without the level of experience and qualifications that external hires would be expected to demonstrate. Consideration should be given to how this is communicated to the wider employee group, particularly the senior non-family employees of the company. Equally, it is important that family employees are seen to be capable of taking on and holding roles within the company, and to that end normal employment practices such as appraisals, feedback and actions to manage under-performance should also be in place.

Other areas: In addition to the creation of an employment policy for family members, there are several other key areas that should be considered as potentially being within the remit of a family employment committee, including policies in the following areas:

- **Employment of spouses and partners:** For some families, the employment of spouses or partners is seen as a positive benefit. It does, however, contain certain risks that need to be managed through the creation of a policy. Employment of one family member's spouse or partner might cause difficulties regarding other family members and their partners or spouses; it may even affect wider relationships when it comes to the management of performance in role, and decisions that affect pay or promotion or even access to information or involvement in family business discussions. Whether this is to do with reality or is based more on perceptions, the existence of a policy to cover these situations may assist. Where a policy on the employment of spouses is developed it should cover the same issues as for other employees, family or not. Importantly, it should make clear who is involved in decisions affecting the terms of employment.
- **Support for family members setting up new business ventures:** Some family businesses will include a restriction in the employment conditions of family directors or senior employees that precludes them becoming involved in activities outside the family business and wealth. Others will pay a premium to family directors or senior employees in recognition of the limits that such employment places on them.

  Some family members will choose not to go into the family business and will seek career or business opportunities on their own. Where a family member seeks to set up their own business, the family will face a choice as to how much involvement there should be from the family and the family business. The family member can be left to pursue their opportunity on their own or alternatively the family could seek to provide support, and may even become involved as a minority investor or a joint venture partner.

d. Membership

Membership will typically comprise two family members and one, or possibly two, independent members who would bring an appropriate level of skills and experience.

The requirement for one or two independent members should be driven by the scope of the committee's activities. Where the activities are limited to employment issues within the family business, one individual with strong HR experience might suffice. Where, however, the focus also covers setting up new business ventures by family members, a broader skill set is likely to be required, and it may not be possible to source both of these from one person.

The experience of independent members of the committee is important as the individuals should, on the one hand, bring the skills and experience to establish a robust approach to the issues based on sound practice, and on the other bring an independence of viewpoint that should be reassuring to the key stakeholders in the decisions reached by the committee – family members employed in the business, family members not employed in the business, and non-family members working in the business.

Of the two family members, there is some benefit in having one who does not work in the family business. This should balance the perspectives of family members who do and do not work in the business, and should allow the views of both to be adequately represented on the issues.

The two family members of the employment committee should be elected by the family council, with the independent member or members being nominated by the family council.

e. Chair

The family council will appoint the chair from the two family members. This is an important decision given the sensitivities surrounding family members working in the family business.

f. Meetings and sundries

Proceeding of the committee and minutes of its meetings should be shared with the family council, and possibly the board of directors of the family business. Clearly, from time to time sensitive matters will be discussed, and the chair of the committee will need to agree with the respective chairs of the family council and family business board how these should be handled.

KEY POINTS

The following points are likely to need discussion in relation to the role and purpose of a family employment committee:

Balance between family and non-family: The nature of the balance between, and/or the involvement of, family and non-family directors and employees is likely to drive the approach taken. For example, where a family firm is strongly dominated at board and senior management levels by members of the family, then those members will closely control decisions about the future. The form of governance is likely to be relatively informal, and it's not unusual to see a reasonably large number of family members employed, in a variety of posts, both full-time and part-time.

Contrast that with a family firm with strong non-family representation at board and/or senior management levels. In such situations it rapidly becomes clear that the interests and treatment of family and non-family individuals will need to be understood and met with a greater degree of formality, certainty and clarity in the governance arrangements and policies in use by the firm.

Family/non-family involvement in governance arrangements: The balance in this area will need to be reflected in the determination regarding decision-making powers over appointments of family members into the management of the family business and wealth, as there is a clear risk that decisions cut across the more obvious and natural forms of governance.

Goals and objectives: It's crucially important that the committee has clarity around the strategic goals and objectives towards which it is working and that underpin its existence and the focus of its work. From this, a clear family employment and/or personnel policy can be established. A key part of this is the principles that will support its work. For example, is there an overriding commitment to meritocracy in decision making around appointments or in respect of the development of family members? Is there a leaning towards or against family involvement? Is there to be parity between family and non-family employees in areas of remuneration, compensation and performance management?

Spouses and in-laws: Within the discussion and creation of a family employment policy, topics such as the employment of spouses and in-laws can cause some difficulty. Clarity as to the basis on which such family members can be employed is important, as inconsistent treatment or decision making here can be a ready source of disagreement in the future.

Suitability of family members: Not all members of the family will want to be, or will be capable of being, family employees. Some family members may wish to pursue wider or different interests; others may wish to do so in the short term. Some may change their minds in due course and want to come into the family business. Some families find it helpful to provide clarity regarding how they will support family members wishing to pursue wider or other interests. For others, such family members are on their own. Other families may choose to provide support, but outside of the family's joint interests. And still others will seek to support entrepreneurial activity from the family's wealth as it brings future growth potential within the family's wealth net.

While all of the above have their pros and cons, an agreed and consistent approach on how the family will treat such situations is likely to be helpful. And yet we find that many families, particularly in the early stages of development, don't set this out, thus storing up potential difficulties for later.

4.13 Audit and risk committee

a. Introduction

While much has been written about the requirements for audit and risk committees for quoted public companies and, to a lesser degree, companies just below quoted size, there is little material on audit and risk committees in relation to family wealth.

The challenge for family-owned businesses is, however, acute:

> *Weaknesses in governance systems of family businesses are most evident in internal controls, internal audit and risk management. Since many family businesses are managed by the founders or their children, the control environment is largely tailored to their needs. The problem: the controls do not grow along with the company, as the business becomes more complex.*[21]

This section covers the potential circumstances for, and role of, an audit and risk committee, from the perspective of the family, the family business and wealth, and the entirety of its affairs, rather than that of individual elements of the family's wealth or wealth structure.

Taking this approach means that there is potential for overlap with the audit and risk committee provision or requirement within the family business (should there be one) and also any audit and risk committee capability within the investment function of the family office.

The point, though, of looking at this from a whole family perspective is to assess whether a sufficiently broad view is taken of the family's affairs, whether there is sufficient coordination of approach, and whether there are gaps.

We draw upon guidance for larger companies, but also other entities such as charities, to inform the discussion for families and their wealth.

b. Role

The main responsibilities, at a high level, of an audit and risk committee are set out in Table 9, with a more detailed description of the responsibilities of the two committees following. Depending on the nature and scale of the family wealth, a decision can be taken whether to have a single committee or two separate ones. For most families a single, joint committee would be expected to be sufficient.

Table 9. Audit and risk committee – areas of responsibility

Audit	Risk
• Ensuring the integrity of the financial reporting and audit process • Monitoring internal control systems	• Making recommendations on the level of risk appetite • Overseeing the process for the identification and management of risk

More detailed responsibilities of the two committees if separately constituted are as follows:

- **Audit committee:**[22]
  - monitoring the integrity of the financial statements and any formal announcements relating to financial performance;
  - reviewing internal financial controls and, unless there is a separate board risk committee, reviewing the company's internal risk controls and risk management systems;
  - monitoring and reviewing the effectiveness of the internal audit function;
  - making recommendations to the board in relation to the appointment, re-appointment and removal of the external auditor and approving the remuneration and terms of engagement of the auditor;
  - reviewing the auditor's independence and objectivity; and
  - developing and implementing the non-audit services policy.
- **Risk committee:**[23]
  - advising the board on the company's overall risk appetite, tolerance and strategy, and the principal and emerging risks the company is willing to take in order to achieve its long-term objectives;

- advising the board on the likelihood and impact of the principal risks materialising and the management and mitigation of the principal risks to reduce their incidence or impact;
- advising the board on the risk aspects of proposed changes to strategy and strategic transactions;
- in relation to internal controls and risk management systems, overseeing and seeking suitable assurance regarding, *inter alia*:
  - the risk exposures of the company;
  - the adequacy and effectiveness of the company's processes and procedures;
  - the company's capability to identify and manage new and emerging risks;
  - the effectiveness and relative costs and benefits of particular controls;
  - the company's ability to reduce the likelihood and impact of risks materialising; and
  - the appropriateness of the company's values and culture and reward systems for managing risks and internal controls, and the extent to which culture and values are embedded.

c. Membership

On membership of the committee, there are a number of issues to consider, as below.[24]

Industry sector: The industry sector and the activities across the family enterprise and wealth will drive the focus of the committee. Matters such as the regulatory environment for the industry or activities, the ownership structure and the scale of the family wealth and enterprise will all have a bearing on the approach taken to membership.

Constitution: Should the committee include independent members? For families considering this, such a requirement might feel overbearing, particularly if there is no experience of independent board members (even on the family company board). Yet the question of independence should still be considered even if the approach to be taken is not to include truly independent members.

An alternative approach, albeit not one that can be considered equivalent, would be to draw membership of the committee from different parts of the family and family wealth structure; this might at least bring a degree of different thinking. To the extent that independent members are not recruited, recognition will need to be given to the conflicts of interest that arise from the other roles the committee members fulfil within the family enterprise.

Experience: For the audit committee element, there should be a member with recent and relevant financial experience. Across the committee as a whole, there should be adequate experience amongst the members.

The above points deal with the core membership; however, it would be appropriate for a number of other role holders to be regular attendees. These might include the CEO and/or finance director of the family business, the CEO or CIO of the family office, and any chief risk officer or similar. The audit partner of the family business audit firm would also be expected to attend from time to time.

d. Chair

In the absence of an independent member within the committee, the chair should be elected from the membership of the committee. It might make sense for the role to be given to the chair of the family council, particularly where that individual is not the chair of the board of the family business.

e. Meetings and sundries

In terms of meetings and sundries the following should be borne in mind:

- There should be clear terms of reference.
- Three meetings per annum might normally suffice.
- Minutes should be taken and circulated to board members and

other relevant bodies within the family governance structure, and any other reporting requirement should be agreed and included in the terms of reference.

KEY POINTS

The following points are likely to need discussion in relation to the role and purpose of an audit and risk committee:

Is the committee required? If so, should there be a joint committee or should they be separate? Given that audit and risk matters will be covered at the family business level and are also likely to be covered if there is a family office, a legitimate question to be asked is whether an audit and risk committee is required at the overall family level.

Much will depend on the scale and complexity of the family's affairs, but also the attitude of the family. Given that the role of the committee at this level is to look right across the entirety of the family's affairs, it is not a given that coverage at family business and family office level will suffice, so careful consideration regarding the approach is merited.

A further key criterion will be the nature of the industry or industries in which a family business operates. Where these are heavily regulated, additional audit and risk coverage may be appropriate.

Role: As stated above, the function of an audit and risk committee, at this level, is to look right across the family affairs. Matters not covered by the audit and risk committees of the family business and family office might include the following:

- reporting within the family governance framework, including the family assembly and council, and adherence to and operation of the family governance framework;
- off-balance sheet transactions, transactions in personal names or assets held in trust;
- cyber and personal security risks;
- reputation and information risks; and
- family succession and wealth continuity and growth at a strategic level.

Composition, formality and engagement: The two key issues regarding composition are, first, whether to have members of the committee who are independent of the family and, secondly, the level of expertise available within the family enterprise structure. We have added the issues of formality and engagement here, as one approach might be to establish an informal, loosely engaged group. Clearly this comes with risk, as the potential issues for a family can be considerable and deserve serious consideration.

4.14 Family code of conduct

a. Introduction

A family code of conduct aims to document the agreed ways in which a family will act, whether in pursuit of the aims and objectives of the family enterprise or in the management of the family's affairs, and whether in internal meetings and processes or in relation to external parties.

Having a family code of conduct recognises that, even though the family has a shared purpose, vision and values, circumstances are such that individual interests, preferences and expectations can and will cause differences of opinion and possibly conflict within a family enterprise.

Such issues are less likely to arise in an owner-managed first-generation family, and still relatively unlikely as the second generation passes into adulthood and comes into the business and/or family wealth, as the founding generation still exerts considerable influence.

Consequently, families in the first and second generation may not develop codes of conduct. Yet this is precisely the time at which it is perhaps easiest and most valuable to do so. With the passing of the founding generation and the growth of family branches and generations, the informal control of the founder can quickly dissipate. Third- and fourth-generation families will be multi-branch, with many in-laws bringing new influences to the family; family members spread around the globe, some working in the business, some not; different levels of shareholdings; and different dependency on the value generated by the family business. And that's before considering those family members who decide to pursue their own independent path or those who perhaps fall foul of the temptations of wealth and its trappings.

Clearly, creating and maintaining a code of conduct does not guarantee that difficulties will not arise, and where they do, the family arbitration committee might be called upon. Hopefully, however, a code of conduct can act as a signalling system for future difficulties that will enable a family to intercept and manage issues before they become harmful. Whereas the family arbitration committee is about dealing with issues once they've arisen, the family code of conduct seeks to pre-empt them.

b. Role

We have highlighted the delicate yet complex nature of family enterprises in many different places within this book. While it is easy to think of the family enterprise as a unit or entity in itself, it is just an aggregation of many individuals, with all of the strengths, opportunities, issues and challenges that they bring. The code of conduct needs, therefore, to address issues relating to individuals as well as those that arise and exist between family members.

While much of the content of a code of conduct will relate to matters within the family, it is important to acknowledge that the family doesn't exist in isolation from the outside world. Its code of conduct needs to address that fact.

While there are many ties that can help to bind a family together, a number of factors, as discussed above, can bring about difficulties, issues and challenges:

- individual family members being treated differently;
- individual family members playing different roles;
- different family members having different attitudes, for example towards risk or contribution, or in respect of reward or responsibility; or
- individual family members behaving differently, for example

through communication, towards other family members or employees, or in relation to the external environment.

These are factors that exist in almost every family and family enterprise, and are not necessarily harmful. Yet if not managed, discussed, explained or dealt with, a perception of unfairness can arise, which can lead to difficulties:

- Different opportunities, roles or reward can give rise to a sense of unequal or inconsistent treatment, or a sense that the family has not fulfilled its obligations to a particular family member.
- Powers over, or involvement in, decision making for some can make others feel excluded or less important.

A code of conduct seeks to articulate how the family and family members will act and deal with difficulties that arise.

c. Content

Individual matters: A code of conduct will contain a number of provisions pertaining to individuals:

- **Confidentiality:** Perhaps the primary item to be included in a code of conduct will be the requirement to maintain confidentiality of family and family member affairs. With the advent of social media, there are so many more channels through which information can come into the public domain that clear governance framework terms for the management and transmission of information are very important. It is not at all unusual these days for families to receive regular training and updates around managing information and reputation, as well as security briefings in respect of themselves and their property.
- **Personal conduct:** Closely linked to the requirement for confidentiality is the issue of personal conduct. The simple fact is that stories regarding the conduct of wealthy families make good headlines. And it's not just about the individual family member; it links to family, friends and those with whom family members might have relationships. Social media, again, has made the issue of personal conduct a bigger challenge.

  While the family code of conduct might not go into huge

levels of detail about the specifics of personal conduct, families increasingly have to discuss and draw a line about what and what isn't expected, and decide when is the right time to discuss the matter.

- **Use and/or gifts of shares:** For family members who own shares in the family business, agreements might be entered into regarding the uses to which such shares may be put. While such matters may be included in the family code of conduct, it is not unusual for these to be subject to legally binding restrictions regarding the ownership of the shares (eg, in a family ownership or shareholders' agreement). Restrictions may be placed on the ability to gift shares, whether that be to other family members or to charity. There may also be restrictions on family shares being pledged or charged in support of borrowing facilities.
- **Exploiting opportunities for personal gain:** Family members will come to possess a wide range of information that could, if mishandled, allow personal gain to arise. Codes of conduct will typically include undertakings that such opportunities will not be exploited, and may cover a wide range of other conflict of interest situations.
- **Exposure to financial leverage:** Particularly for family members who rely on the family enterprise or wealth for their financial wellbeing, this is an important clause since, should excessive financial leverage occur, the family enterprise or wealth is likely to be the only source of alleviation. This clause may also extend to the way in which family members manage their financial affairs more widely, and include the agreed use of certain professional and financial advisers, thereby enabling the family to maintain a consistent approach to their affairs.
- **Other commitments:** A wide range of matters can be included, for example pre-nuptial agreements.

Family matters: A code of conduct is likely to contain the following with regard to family matters:

- support for the family vision and ethos;
- a commitment to act in line with and uphold the family values;
- support for other family members;

- a commitment to respect the roles that family members have, the basis upon which roles are obtained or appointments made, and the abilities of the person in role;
- a commitment to consensus-based decision making; and
- a commitment to use the agreed channels where disagreement with family matters or individuals arise.

External matters: The code of conduct might include reference to the way in which family members handle relationships with staff, whether working in the family business or for individual family members. This would also be likely to cover relationships with senior management in the family business and professional external advisers.

There is an increasing body of legislation affecting roles in the workplace, so thought should be given to how a particular piece of legislation is handled and whether it should apply more widely than just in relation to positions held in the family enterprise. Matters covered include:

- bribery and corruption;
- fraud;
- gifts and hospitality;
- competition;
- health and safety;
- modern slavery; and
- the environment.

The limitations of family codes of conduct do have to be recognised. They tend to work well with supportive, compliant family members, but in truth these members aren't the likely source of difficulty for families. The family members who take a less attitudinally supportive approach are the ones least likely to comply. For these reasons, a discussion about the form of the commitments and the level of enforceability needs to be held.

d. Drafting and maintaining

While the family council may well be responsible for overseeing the drafting of the code of conduct, in relation to the full breadth of the family its maintenance is more likely to fall to the family assembly.

"The limitations of family codes of conduct do have to be recognised. They tend to work well with supportive, compliant family members, but in truth these members aren't the likely source of difficulty for families. The family members who take a less attitudinally supportive approach are the ones least likely to comply."

However, family members will take on different roles across the ownership, working and family member axes, so the code of conduct will only apply in respect of the part relevant to each family member.

If, for example, a family member is employed in the family enterprise, those aspects of the code of conduct relevant to being employed may feature in their employment contract. And, as mentioned earlier, commitments relevant to being an owner in the family enterprise may be included in the ownership agreement. Perhaps the most tricky part relates to just being a family member, for which no legal document exists. This is where the standing of the family governance framework comes in, although in reality the level of commitment around the code of conduct as it applies to just a family member is unlikely to be more than a moral one.

e. Breach

Where the code of conduct is backed up by a legal agreement, the consequences of a breach can be set out in the relevant documentation and would link to other policies – the employment contract and policy or the family shareholder or ownership agreement. For other matters, resolution may be referred to the family arbitration committee. What happens in relation to breach of the family code of conduct can be set out either in the code of conduct itself or, possibly, in the terms of reference of the family arbitration committee.

KEY POINTS

There are two relatively simple, but paradoxically quite complex, discussion points in relation to the family code of conduct:

- what is included in the code of conduct; and
- how enforceable are its terms.

5. Corporate governance elements

5.1 Management board of the holding company[25]

a. Introduction

Alongside the family council (the body representing the family owners) the management board of the holding company is another of the pivotal elements of the family governance framework.[26]

Whereas the family council is the key body in respect of the governance of the family owners, their affairs and interests, the management board of the holding company is the key body in respect of the governance of the family business.

With the potential for overlap between family members, shareholders, directors, senior managers and even employees in family businesses, the influences and pressures these groups can come under have the potential to pull them in many directions. Having strong business governance, therefore, can be extremely important.

We know that in many family businesses the owners are also directors of the business, sitting on the management board. It is vital to distinguish the role of a shareholder/owner from that of a management board director, even if sometimes a single person or group of people might hold both roles.

Recognising that family-owned businesses come in all shapes and sizes, from some of the world's largest and well-known businesses to small owner-managed ones, we will explore in some depth the range of guidance available from corporate governance codes on the relationship between shareholders and the management board.

The *G20/OECD Principles of Corporate Governance* from 2015 set out two main elements that make up a corporate governance framework, providing real clarity about what corporate governance is and what it aims to deliver:[27]

- a set of relationships between a company's management, board, shareholders and other stakeholders; and

- a structure through which the objectives of the company are set and the means of attaining those objectives and monitoring performance are determined.

Taking this a step further, although applying to larger companies, the nature of the relationship between the management board and owners is well summarised by this extract from the UK Corporate Governance Code:[28]

> *Corporate governance is the system by which companies are directed and controlled.*
>
> *Boards of directors are responsible for the governance of their companies. The shareholders' role in governance is to appoint the directors and the auditors and to satisfy themselves that an appropriate governance structure is in place. The responsibilities of the board include setting the company's strategic aims, providing the leadership to put them into effect, supervising the management of the business and reporting to shareholders on their stewardship. The board's actions are subject to laws, regulations and the shareholders in general meeting.*

The role played by the management board is a critical one in that it has responsibility for the delivery of the strategy and plans of the company as well as its results.

In family-owned enterprises, the management board will be responsible for the management and performance of what could be a very significant proportion of the family's wealth and which may well be the primary source of the family's income. Therefore, a well-articulated and well-functioning relationship between the management board and family council (the owners) is very important.

The management board is appointed by the owners of the company (the family council) to conduct the day-to-day affairs of the company, and is accountable to the family council for the results it achieves. As owners, however, the family council cannot and should not become engaged in the day-to-day running of the company.

The relationship between the shareholders, the directors and the company will be set out in the constitution documents of the company. In the UK and a number of other countries around the world the two key documents are the memorandum of association and the articles of association.

As stated earlier, family-owned enterprises span a very wide range of size and complexity, from small owner-managed businesses to some of the largest enterprises in the world's economies.[29] The same basic principle of splitting ownership and management applies in all these cases; however, the manner in which the relationship is structured and the standards to which it is required to operate vary widely.

b. Role

While the duties and role of boards are, in general terms, very similar, differences in specific duties and roles can and do occur. These might be the result of the legal jurisdiction in which the company is incorporated, the nature and size of the company, the type of company being used, or specific clauses in the constitution documents of the company.

Issues relating to company type, legal jurisdiction and constitution documents can only be explored once the specifics are known. We can, however, examine some of the issues that arise according to the size and status of the company, as below.

Issues arising from governance codes for listed companies: Companies listed on stock exchanges around the world will be subject to the listing requirements of the relevant exchange. The UK Corporate Governance Code 2018 is built around a set of principles organised under five headings, and while there is some flexibility in the application of the principles, this is backed up by a regime of 'comply or explain' provisions and supporting guidance:

- board leadership and company purpose;
- division of responsibilities;
- composition, succession and evaluation;
- audit, risk and internal control; and
- remuneration.

Issues arising from governance of unlisted companies: Generally, much less time has been invested in the creation of corporate governance guidance for unlisted companies. The material below, including the Principles, is drawn from the 2010 *ecoDa Corporate Governance Guidance and Principles for Unlisted Companies in Europe.*[30]

Two quotes in the report from working group members highlight the importance of this guidance:

> *"The corporate governance needs of such [unlisted] companies have hitherto been relatively neglected by governance experts and policy-makers alike. The principles of good governance ... are practical and pragmatic. The manner in which they should be applied will depend on the circumstances of each company and judgment of individual Boards."*[31]

> *"Family businesses, most of which are privately held, will benefit from thinking proactively about how best to set up their corporate governance."*[32]

In *Corporate Governance*, ecoDa set out 14 principles in two phases:[33]

Phase 1 principles: Corporate governance principles applicable to all unlisted companies

Principle 1: *Shareholders should establish an appropriate constitutional and governance framework for the company.*

Principle 2: *Every company should strive to establish an effective board, which is collectively responsible for the long-term success of the company, including the definition of corporate strategy. However, an interim step on the road to an effective (and independent) board may be the creation of an advisory board.*

Principle 3: *The size and composition of the board should reflect the scale and complexity of the company's activities.*

"For me, these nine principles represent a relatively straightforward, achievable, progressive approach to establishing good corporate governance. They recognise the need for flexibility but at the same time set out a clear definition of what good governance should look like."

Principle 4: *The board should meet sufficiently regularly to discharge its duties, and be supplied in a timely manner with appropriate information.*

Principle 5: *Levels of remuneration should be sufficient to attract, retain and motivate executives and non-executives of the quality required to run the company successfully.*

Principle 6: *The board is responsible for risk oversight and should maintain a sound system of internal control to safeguard shareholders' investment and company assets.*

Principle 7: *There should be a dialogue between the board and the shareholders based on the mutual understanding of objectives. The board as a whole has responsibility for ensuring that a satisfactory dialogue with shareholders takes place. The board should not forget that all shareholders have to be treated equally.*

Principle 8: *All directors should receive induction on joining the board and should regularly update and refresh their skills and knowledge.*

Principle 9: *Family-controlled companies should establish family governance mechanisms that promote coordination and mutual understanding amongst family members, as well as organise the relationship between family governance and corporate governance.*

For me, these nine principles represent a relatively straightforward, achievable, progressive approach to establishing good corporate governance. They recognise the need for flexibility but at the same time set out a clear definition of what good governance should look like.

In respect of family-controlled companies, Principle 9 is important as it highlights the need for family governance mechanisms, emphasising two key elements:

- coordination and understanding amongst family members; and
- the relationship between family and corporate governance.

Unlisted companies already on the journey to establishing a corporate governance framework can benchmark themselves against these principles, while companies at an earlier stage of the journey can use it as a roadmap.

The Phase 2 principles set out below provide the next step, bridging closer to the sorts of governance expectations of larger listed companies.[34]

Phase 2 principles: Corporate governance principles applicable to large and/or more complex unlisted companies

Principle 10: *There should be a clear division of responsibilities at the head of the company between running the board and the running of the company's business. No one individual should have unfettered powers of decision.*

Principle 11: *Board structures vary according to national regulatory requirements and business norms. However, all boards should contain directors with a sufficient mix of competencies and experiences. No single person (or small group of individuals) should dominate board decision making.*

Principle 12: *The board should establish appropriate board committees in order to allow a more effective discharge of its duties.*

Principle 13: *The board should undertake a periodic appraisal of its own performance and that of each individual director.*

Principle 14: *The board should present a balanced and understandable assessment of the company's position and prospects for external stakeholders, and establish a suitable programme of stakeholder engagement.*

Issues arising in corporate governance of family businesses: The amount of guidance available for governance in family-owned businesses is lower than for larger companies, which is perhaps surprising given the scale of family businesses in the global economy.

The first code, as such, was created in 2004 in Germany – *The Governance Code for Family Businesses* by Kommission Governance Kodex für Familienunternehmen. It is now in its third iteration, from May 2015.[35] The preamble to the Code highlights its importance:

> *Family businesses not only represent the majority of businesses and sources of employment in our country; they also have a special responsibility for society. Through the multi-generational orientation of their business model and the long-term approach that it involves, they have a commitment to deal responsibly with their employees and all other stakeholders. Because of this, the property rights are also accompanied by a special responsibility on the part of the business-owning family to organise itself in a way that will ensure a modern, sustainable approach to business management.*

The Code, at section 1 sub-sections 1.1–1.3, suggests that family business owners address three key considerations:

> *1.1 Owners should determine the values and goals to which they feel committed in view of their family ownership and their family business.*
>
> *1.2 In this connection, they should define the extent to which they want to take into account not only the interests of the owner family but also the interests of other stakeholders, in particular the employees and the customers, and to contribute to the development of society through sustainable management.*
>
> *1.3 Owners should also define the importance they attach to maintaining the business as a family-owned business, and the extent to which the interests of the business take precedence over the interests of the ownership collective and the individual interests of the owners.*

These three points are important to reflect on, as they highlight the importance of purpose (including goals and values) and the interests of family and other stakeholders. They closely align with the first two steps I use in approaching the development of a family governance framework, outlined in the Summary section at the end of Part II above.

The Code then sets out considerations regarding family business governance that a family-owned business should implement in its approach to governance, in the following areas:

- structure of owner rights and obligations;
- supervisory body;
- company management;
- measurement and disposition of earnings;
- transferability of ownership, withdrawal from the group of owners;
- family governance; and
- creation and validity of an own-governance code.

Understanding the different roles in a business: The dynamics of family-owned businesses, with family members often playing multiple roles (shareholder, director, senior manager) mean that a family member can have multiple responsibilities, driven by the requirements of the positions that they hold. This can sometimes make it a challenge to achieve the same level of clarity normally seen in the approach to corporate governance in larger companies, as discussed above.

It is therefore worth considering and highlighting the specific rights, duties and/or responsibilities of the various roles in corporate governance that apply to role holders, regardless of the number of roles that a family member holds. Clearly the specifics will depend on the type of company and the jurisdiction of the company's incorporation:

- **General rights of shareholders:**[36]
  - to have secure methods of ownership registration;
  - to convey or transfer shares;
  - to obtain relevant and material information on the company on a timely and regular basis;
  - to participate and vote in general shareholder meetings;
  - to elect and remove members of the board; and
  - to share in the profits of the corporation.
- **General duties of a board:**[37]
  - to be collectively responsible for the long-term success of the company;
  - to provide entrepreneurial leadership of the company within a framework of prudent and effective controls;

  - to set the company's strategic aims;
  - to ensure that the necessary financial and human resources are in place for the company to meet its objectives;
  - to review the performance of management and the board;
  - to set the company's values and standards;
  - to ensure that the obligations to shareholders and others are understood and met;
  - to determine the nature and extent of significant risks and maintain sound risk management and internal control systems; and
  - to delegate authority to management and monitor the implementation of policies, strategies and operational plans.
- **General duties of a director:**[38]
  - to act within the company's powers;
  - to act in a way the director considers (in good faith) is most likely to promote the success of the company for the benefit of its members as a whole, having regard to the following matters (specifically identified in the legislation):
    - the likely consequences of any decision in the long term;
    - the interests of the company's employees;
    - the need to foster the company's business relationships with suppliers, customers and others;
    - the impact of the company's operations on the community and the environment;
    - the desirability of the company maintaining a reputation for high standard business conduct; and
    - the need to act fairly as between the members of the company.
  - to exercise independent judgement;
  - to exercise reasonable care, skill and diligence;
  - to avoid conflicts (or possible conflicts) between the interests of the director and those of the company;
  - not to accept benefits from third parties by reason of being a director or doing anything as a director; and
  - to declare any interest in a proposed transaction or arrangement.
- **General duties of management:**[39]
  - to see to the day-to-day running of the company, in line with

the strategic and business plans, and budgets approved by the board of directors;
- to act in line with powers delegated by the board;
- to make recommendations to the board of directors on strategy and business plans;
- to implement decisions of the board of directors; and
- to provide information to the board to enable it to discharge its duties.

Family issues: When the roles are listed out clearly, as above, all can seem straightforward. With family-owned businesses, however, in practice things are rarely so simple, so it's worth considering some of the issues that may arise:

- There is a risk that family attachment, legacy or emotions may compromise the clarity seen when the various roles are completely separated.
- Clear and open communication channels may become compromised by certain family members who hold multiple roles overlooking the need to pass on and share information with others who do not hold the same roles.
- Lines of accountability and responsibility may become blurred as corporate governance standards are applied more loosely.
- Minority shareholder interests may not be fully looked after.
- The appointment of family members to the board may compromise the quality of the board or may not allow for the recruitment of directors with the key skill sets required.
- Family dynamics may cause the avoidance of issues and potentially create a lack of decisiveness.
- Conflicts of interest may arise, and these may not be handled as robustly as desired.
- Given the importance of the family, performance management and succession issues may not be fully considered by the board.

c. Membership

Company law in the relevant jurisdiction will ordinarily dictate the minimum number of directors required on a board of directors. In the UK, for example, for a private limited company the statutory minimum requirement is currently one, and there is no statutory maximum. A company's articles of association may well stipulate a minimum and maximum number of directors required for the company.

Rather than being driven by a target number of directors, however, consideration regarding membership of the board should flow from the requirements and duties of the board in relation to the company:

- The board and its committees should have the appropriate balance of skills, experience, independence and knowledge of the company to enable them to discharge their respective duties and responsibilities effectively.
- There should be a formal, rigorous and transparent procedure for the appointment of new directors to the board.
- All directors should be able to allocate sufficient time to the company to discharge their responsibilities effectively.
- All directors should receive induction on joining the board and should regularly update and refresh their skills and knowledge.

For smaller, owner-managed or sibling-owned family businesses, the directors are likely to be drawn from a narrow group at the heart of the family. For larger, more complex family businesses the number, breadth and experience of the board of directors is likely to be greater, and may involve independent, non-family directors. Where companies are listed, the corporate governance rules of the jurisdiction in which the company is listed are likely to set down certain stipulations regarding the number and composition of the board of directors.

The right of appointment and removal of directors is a power, in UK company law, that is vested in the shareholders of a company. In family governance terms, this is likely to be the family council where it fulfils the shareholder body role.

Given the level of control that the board exercises over a company's strategy, direction and plans, the power of appointment and removal of directors is one of the key powers exercisable by the shareholders. It is not, therefore, unusual for the precise arrangements for the appointment and removal of directors to be tightly drawn and embedded in the company's articles of association.

d. Chair

The chair of the board is a critical position in the governance structure given that his or her primary role is to manage the business of the board. This is quite distinct from the role of the chief executive, which involves running the business itself.

The chair's responsibilities will typically include the following:

- planning and managing board meetings (including preparation of agendas, circulation of papers in sufficient time and preparation and approval of minutes);
- managing the conduct of business at board meetings (including ensuring that sufficient time is set aside for discussion of all agenda items, particularly those of a strategic nature, and that decisions taken are clearly recorded);
- clarifying board and management responsibilities;
- reviewing the effectiveness of the board and individual directors; and
- ensuring that the communication with shareholders is effective.

The company's articles of association will contain any specific requirements regarding the chair.

e. Meetings and sundries

The formal rules relating to the conduct of board meetings will largely be found in the articles of association of the company. The only company law requirement (in the UK) is to keep minutes.

While the articles of association are likely to contain provisions with regard to the items listed below, this leaves a significant amount of latitude in the way in which the management board is actually run. Typically, the smaller the company the more informal the board proceedings.

This issue of informality in smaller family-owned businesses can represent quite a challenge as companies grow, or when they seek or need to develop a stronger governance framework.

Common provisions are as follows:

- directors taking decisions;
- quorum for meetings;
- calling meetings and participating in meetings;
- chairing arrangements and casting vote;
- conflicts of interest; and
- records of decisions kept.

KEY POINTS

Corporate governance and the stages of family businesses: Many family businesses start out as owner managed, with one family member clearly being the founder. In this scenario, the three major dynamics of family governance – ownership, family and business – are all consolidated under the one person. Corporate governance at this stage tends not to be a major consideration, beyond meeting the legal requirements of the jurisdiction of the company's incorporation and conducting any business that requires the board's approval.

Figure 9. Stages of family businesses

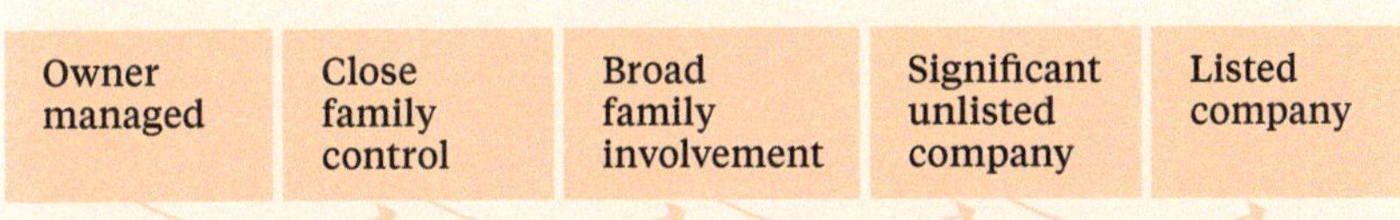

Source: Author.

Equally, a significant number of family businesses start out with a small number of principals, often from the same family, but sometimes with a very small group of owners/founders.

As the family and company grow, things will develop beyond being under the control of just the founder(s). Examples of such developments are as follows:

- The founder(s) need(s) to recruit senior management to the company to support its growth.

- The business grows in complexity such that the founder(s) can no longer manage the business single-handedly.
- The next generation from the founder(s) begin to take over responsibility for the day-to-day running of the business, and start to occupy the senior management positions of the company.
- The founder(s) share(s) ownership of the family business with their children, some of whom work in the family business and some of whom don't.

At this stage, control of the ownership and management is likely to remain within the core of the family or families. It is unlikely that there will be a significant formal role for the board.

As the family and company develop further, certain changes may drive a need for greater board involvement, and a mix of executive and non-executive directors:

- The ownership of the company is more widely distributed across the family or families. Not all owners can sit on the board and thus some owners are 'represented' on the board.
- The family or families have grown significantly. The existence of different branches (at the cousins stage) means that the control exerted by the founder(s) has been lost.
- There are non-family owners, possibly external equity holders or senior management.
- The family business is now a complex operation that would benefit from the involvement of external expertise.

The next stage to which family-owned companies might progress is where they are significant and complex concerns. At this stage there is a need for a much clearer separation of the senior management from the governance functions and role of the board, and/or there is a separation of some of the owners from the board. As a significant enterprise the company may demonstrate one or more of the following characteristics, which drive the need for a more professionalised board with a greater, if not majority, non-family involvement:

- external, non-family, venture capital or private equity investors;

- support from debt capital markets;
- regulation or an increase in profile sufficient to involve significant non-executive input; and/or
- a management function that is onerous and significant enough to require external, non-executive support in the areas of nomination and remuneration, audit and risk.

Benefits of corporate governance for family businesses: As discussed above, not all family businesses require a formal board structure, and in the early stages of a family business it is highly unlikely that the company will have a formal approach to board meetings. From this starting position, the development of a more structured approach to corporate governance can meet with a number of objections from an individual who is an owner/manager (see below). Yet the natural tendency when discussing family governance can be to suggest a more formalised role for the board. Not only should the views of the owner/manager be assessed, but the natural governance of the family should also be considered and discussed to see whether the formalising of the board's role could add value to the governance of the family, as it might in fact have the opposite effect.

These are the sorts of objections that might be encountered:
- "A board of directors will constrain me."
- "I risk a loss of control and I might be stuck with a board of directors."
- "It will slow down decision making."
- "It will expose family and company issues to external people."

While a response can be made to each of these points, beyond that, a professionalised board offers a number of benefits:
- **Better decision making:** Governance within a company is primarily concerned with the structures, processes and procedures by which the business of the company is conducted. Given the role of the board, the development of a broader and deeper body of expertise, with the time and information to consider matters more fully should, if well managed, allow

better decisions to be made for the benefit of the company and its owners.

A founder is unlikely to be able to be able to do all of this on their own as a company grows in size and complexity.

- **Safeguarding the position of a wider group of owners:** The owners of family businesses are typically not readily able to sell their shares. Not only are they normally limited to selling to other family members; it is also not unusual for there to be restrictive shareholders' agreements in place.

  As the number of family owners increases it becomes less likely that all owners will have a seat on the board, posing a risk to them in terms of the strategy of the company.

  A strengthened board can therefore play a strong role in protecting their interests and the value of their holding in the company.
- **Corporate reputation:** Company law, laws relating to the duties of companies and their directors, and governance codes relating to unlisted companies, are increasingly recognising the need for companies to have regard to the interests of stakeholders beyond the narrow confines of the company itself.

  As companies grow in size and complexity, the interest of these external parties in the company will continue to grow. For much larger private companies there have been a number of well-publicised cases where the wider community's interest appears not to have been sufficiently safeguarded, and this has affected not only the reputation of the company but also the principal and the family behind the company.

  A strengthened board, with an appropriate focus on these external influences and pressures, is more likely to safeguard the reputation and ultimately the success of the company.
- **Checks and balances:** Corporate governance allows for the wider development of a system of checks and balances to safeguard the interests of the various parties within a company. A well-designed corporate governance model should provide a high level of transparency and accountability, which ensures that decision making is not concentrated in the hands of one person and should assist in management of conflicts of interest.

Whether through reserved powers, delegation of authority, independent directors, the use meetings, resolutions, committee structures, a formal approach to reporting or the management of conflicts of interest, a governance model can be built to recognise the extent and limits of the powers of the various parties and provide an enhanced level of protection for them.

Challenges of implementing corporate governance: As discussed above, a more formal approach to corporate governance in a family-owned business is unlikely to take place until the owner/manager is committed to it. It is only likely to succeed if it develops the natural governance already in place in the family business and is implemented in a dedicated and disciplined manner.

Beyond those two conditions, implementing formal corporate governance can be tackled in a number of different ways, with attendant challenges:

- **A natural phased approach as the family business grows:** On the face of it, a natural evolution of corporate governance as a company grows would seem to be the easiest path. However, a number of challenges can and do arise:
    - **The agency problem:** This arises as external senior managers are employed in the company, and as they seek to influence the performance and strategic development of the company and look for rewards for their efforts, which may not be in alignment with the reward structure that the family wishes to be in place. Senior management may also seek to be appointed as directors of the company, with a seat on the board, which of course gives them a greater say in the formal governance of the company.
    - **The first independent director:** One of the first steps in developing corporate governance in a company is to appoint an independent or non-executive director. However, such appointees are often close associates or friends of the owner/manager, which can give rise to a conflict between the personal relationship and the governance relationship as between the two individuals.

"As the family grows it is likely that the ownership of the company will become more distributed among family members, not all of whom are likely to be working in the business."

  - **An advisory board:** Another approach can be to appoint an advisory board to support the owner/manager or board of the company, which as the name suggests is only able to provide advice. Issues can arise where the advisory board feels its advice is continually ignored, or where the owner/manager feels there is too much interference.
  - **Family shareholders not working in the business:** As the family grows it is likely that the ownership of the company will become more distributed among family members, not all of whom are likely to be working in the business. As the roles separate, so does the nature of the reward for the different family members, and as the nature of reward separates so does the level of interest in the reward. Situations can, however, arise where family shareholders not working in the business have different views about the future of the company from those family members on the board and running the business.
- **Logical model development for corporate governance:** Some family-owned businesses will approach the development of corporate governance on a more structured basis, defining the duties, responsibilities, tasks and functions expected of a board and then recruiting directors to provide the appropriate mix of skills and experience. Yet, this approach can still give rise to a number of implementation challenges:
  - **Creating a clear remit for the board, and separating what it does from both the owners and management:** On the face of it, creation of a clear remit should be straightforward, as should the delegation of powers from board to senior management. But in practice, in family-owned businesses the owners will seek to retain a number of powers for themselves, including:
    - appointment and dismissal of directors;
    - remuneration of directors;
    - annual setting of company strategy;
    - annual sign-off on business plan and budget;
    - control over acquisitions and disposals; and
    - control over major expenditure above a certain figure or major contractual commitment.

The retention of certain powers, while done with the best of intentions, does introduce friction into the corporate governance in terms of decision-making effectiveness and efficiency.

- **Size and composition of the board:** The questions of how many people should sit on the board and from where they should be drawn will have particular resonance in family-owned businesses. In addition to the expectations of family members and senior management, consideration will need to be given to whether there should be independent directors. Throw in the matter of ensuring that board members have the necessary skill set, and the question of size and mix can become quite complicated:
  - **Skill set:** It is worth drawing up a list of the skills and experience required by members of the board and using this to assess the recruitment of board members, and understanding what this means for the likely number of directors on the board.
  - **Board size:** For an unlisted family company, opinion seems to suggest a board with a minimum of three members and a maximum of between seven and nine.
  - **Board mix:** The consensus regarding the mix of executive and non-executive members is that the non-executive members should be in a majority. The nature of the involvement of family members on the board will need to take into account the level of involvement of the family on the executive side of the business, as well as the nature of the family ownership.

    Where the executive side of the business is fully staffed by professional, non-family management, the non-executive side would be likely to see strong family representation. Where the CEO and possibly a number of the executives are from the family, then one would expect to see non-family independent non-executives.

    Where there are external, non-family shareholders, thought should be given to their representation on the board.

Consideration should also be given to wider diversity issues such as gender, age, ethnicity and cultural backgrounds.

   - **Board evaluation:** The final step is to ensure that there is a board evaluation process in place.

- **A corporate event:** Where a corporate event takes place (eg, external finance raising, shareholder expansion, partial equity sale) the status quo of the corporate governance framework will be disturbed. Not only will the different expectation of the parties have to be catered for, but there are also likely to be different attitudes to the style of corporate governance in place.
- **Separation of ownership and management:** As the ownership and management of a company separates into the hands of different groups of individuals, it is likely that there will be a divergence of opinion and views about the strategic direction and financial objectives of the company.

  With the board and management potentially interested in different outcomes from the owners, inevitably the possibility of conflicting views arises. In this scenario, attention will need to be given to the process for objective-setting to ensure that actions, outcomes and rewards are aligned.

Appointments: The appointment of the chair and other key individuals is critical within the governance framework. Where one or more of the following conditions apply, it is likely that the role of chair will require careful consideration:

- The ownership structure of the family business is well diversified, and/or not all of the owners work in the family business.
- There are non-family owners.
- The senior management of the company is no longer family member dominated.
- The family business is significant in scale or complexity.

Two key questions then need to be answered:

- **Should the chair be a non-family member?** Where a family business is of sufficient size for there to be a professional board

of directors, opinion seems to suggest that where one or other of the chair or CEO of the family business is a family member, then the other should be a non-family member. This flows from the principle of ensuring sufficient checks and balances and the protection of the company's and shareholders' interests.
- **Should the chair be the same person as the chair of the family council?** Where a family business and the interests of the family are of sufficient size and complexity, opinion seems to suggest that the two roles should not be filled by the same family member. While the chair of the family business is concerned with the development of the company, the chair of the family council, which is often the shareholder body, is concerned with the wider interests of the family. In practice this is more likely to apply when a family has grown to a point where the third generation is actively involved in both the family and the family business.

The process for and terms of any appointments to the board should be made clear in writing. One would expect to see the following matters covered:
- length of term of office;
- maximum number of terms;
- remuneration; and
- numbers of meetings.

Guidance on the issue of board representation suggests that the following individuals should not be appointed to the board of the family business, as it is felt likely that they will reduce its objectivity:
- friends and close associates of the owners;
- professional service providers to the company, such as accountants, lawyers and bankers;
- suppliers to the company; and
- individuals where there would be a conflict of interest, including those with inadequate time to be able to properly undertake their role.

5.2 Shareholders' agreement

a. Introduction

The creation of a legally binding agreement between the shareholders of a company can provide the owners with a mechanism for setting out in advance how they will deal with a very wide range of circumstances or eventualities that may befall the company or its owners. The aim of the agreement is to protect the shareholders' rights to the return due from their ownership of the shares, which comes in two forms:

- the rights to any share of the profits that may come in the form of a dividend; and
- the right to their proportion of the value of the company as represented by the portion of the company's shares held.

In relation to a family wealth structure, a shareholders' agreement can be used in respect of any companies within the structure. Although the primary use of a shareholders' agreement would ordinarily be at the main holding company level, for larger, complex groups of companies, a shareholders' agreement may be in place at different levels in the structure, particularly if external shareholders (eg, management) are present in the structure. It can complement the family charter and provide a mechanism for legally embedding certain of its provisions.

A shareholders' agreement can be used to provide protection for the owners of the company, and by extension the management and employees, as well as to enable the owners to document their approach to issues that can often be a source of contention or disagreement in the future.

A major advantage of a shareholders' agreement is that it is not a public document, and thus its provisions can remain confidential between the parties. Clarification of the roles, powers and protections afforded to the various parties should provide for a smoother functioning of the company.

It is helpful to discuss and set out the way these matters will be dealt with in advance, at a time when there is goodwill and positivity between the shareholders.

b. Philosophies and approaches

With many companies formed and regulated according to a standard set of articles of association for the jurisdiction or country under which they are formed, the articles may not set out with the required degree of precision the relationship that is desired between the various parties involved in the governance of the company.

A shareholders' agreement, if created, will sit alongside the articles of association, so a clear understanding of what the two documents are going to contain is required.

Consideration of the agreement should also reflect the context of the ownership of the company – for example:

- Are all of the shareholders siblings?
- Are they family members of the different generations?
- Do the shareholders reflect different branches of the original family, or are they a mix of family and non-family?

The way in which the owners and management of the company, through the directors, intend to interact also needs to be taken into account.

There are a number of scenarios which highlight some of the key ways in which a shareholders' agreement can be focused:

Company shareholders do not intend to take up positions on the board: Rather, they intend to appoint external directors to manage the company. A shareholders' agreement in this scenario would be likely to contain provisions for the protection of the shareholders by making certain decisions and actions of the board subject to positive or negative undertakings.

Positive undertakings include:

- provision of financial information, strategic plans and budgets; and
- pay and pension arrangements for senior staff.

Negative undertakings include:

- not changing the nature of the company's activities;
- not entering new markets, making major investments or disinvestments, or creating subsidiaries; and
- not borrowing or giving security in certain situations.

The shareholders' agreement may also contain provisions regarding the appointment of directors, and likely also the interactions of the shareholders that come up in the scenarios below.

The company has a wide range of family minority shareholders, who are also directors: A shareholders' agreement for this scenario would be likely to contain the following provisions:

- protections for minority shareholders, including arrangements where minority shareholders wish to sell their shares and the process by which this takes place;
- rights of minority shareholders when an offer for the company has been received;
- provisions regarding the death of a shareholder and what happens to the shares in this eventuality, with the position and rights of the executor or surviving spouse being made clear (in these scenarios, thought needs to be given to how the value of the company can be protected – shareholders might take out life policies with supporting cross-option agreements that would use the proceeds to acquire the shares of the surviving shareholder);
- decision making/voting rights at board meetings, often providing protection for the position of the shareholders through the right to appoint (and remove or replace) a specific director;
- details regarding the level of support for certain resolutions – simple majority decisions, higher threshold decisions and unanimous decisions;
- arrangements regarding the appointment and removal of directors; and
- dividend policy.

Company with a majority family shareholder: A shareholders' agreement for this scenario would be likely to contain the following:

- limits or restrictions on the powers of the board of directors, where the majority owner does not sit on the board or where he or she does not have majority representation;
- agreement regarding the appointment and removal of directors;
- provisions regarding any voting rights required to protect the majority shareholder's position;
- provisions regarding the injection of additional funds into the business;
- provisions that prevent minority shareholders frustrating the sale of the business;
- a methodology for valuing the shares and agreeing any discounts to be applied to the share value in the event of sale; and
- non-competition clauses and/or confidentiality agreements.

Company with two shareholders, each owning 50% of the shares: Where a company has two 50% owners and they are the two sole board directors, there is a risk that deadlock could arise at board or ownership level or both. Such situations can be extremely harmful to the company's prospects, and having provisions in place through a shareholders' agreement can save much difficulty and expense down the line. Some of the differences that can arise between shareholders and directors are shown in Table 10.

Table 10. Causes of dispute or deadlock

Between shareholders	Between directors
• Strategy and plans for the business • Financing of the business • Financial return to shareholders • Directors' appointment and removal • Directors' remuneration • Authority levels	• Strategy and plans for the business • Financial performance • Communication and transparency • Power struggles over responsibility or remuneration • Conflicts of interest

The situation can be avoided by structuring the ownership such that it isn't equal (eg, 51:49 or by using different classes of shares) or by appointing a third-party director who doesn't own shares but would have, in effect, a casting vote at board level.

The following options for using a shareholders' agreement are also available, although there are pros and cons to each:

- a clause in the agreement that allows one or the other shareholder to acquire the shares of the other, with provisions for calculating the price at which the transaction might take place; and
- deadlock provisions that set out what is to happen in that event.

KEY POINTS

Notwithstanding the foregoing, the following sections detail, by subject matter, the sorts of provisions that might be contained in a shareholders' agreement.

General rules: The shareholders' agreement may set out arrangements regarding the key advisers and service providers to the company (auditors, bankers, company secretary) and any limits or requirements that need to be met for them to be changed.

Matters requiring specific consent: Items in this section of the shareholders' agreement will include the following:

- delineation of responsibilities with management and the content of any agreements that are required;
- powers retained by shareholders – appointment and removal of directors, appointment or dismissal of key employees, director remuneration;
- right to board representation;
- voting thresholds for certain types of decisions; and
- details of positive or negative undertakings.

Dividend policy: The shareholders' agreement may well contain provisions relating to the company's dividend policy. While shareholders will wish to see these provisions included, as the dividend is one part of the return they can generate from their ownership of the company, it is important that this does not have a harmful impact on the business through over-depletion of its reserves. There may therefore be financial provisions which have to be exceeded for a dividend to be paid.

Raising capital: The shareholders' agreement may well contain provisions relating to the raising of finance, whether through equity or debt. It is likely to require a threshold level of shareholder support, and in the case of a rights issue, will need to contain provisions for what happens where a shareholder does not take up his or her rights.

Share transfer: Provisions relating to the transfer of shares may be included, covering some or all of the following:

- **Transfer between family members:** It is likely that there will be detailed procedures for the sale and transfer of shares between family members. These are likely to contain clauses covering some or all of the following:
  - **Oversight:** Who within the family will oversee the transfer process? This may, for example, fall within the remit of the chair of the family council.
  - **Timetable:** What is the timetable for the process? There may be different timetables and processes to deal with different triggers for a transfer – eg, sale, gift or death.
  - **Notice:** How is notice of the intention to dispose of shares given, and how often can the process be triggered (annually, for example)? There may also be provisions here regarding the number of times a shareholder can make partial reductions, the minimum size of any disposals or a requirement for an entire stake to be sold, as well as restrictions on that family member buying back into the company in due course.
  - **Valuation:** How are the shares put up for sale valued, and over what period does the valuation apply? The procedures may also deal with the issue of any variation to the projected per-share valuation to deal with the size of the shareholding put up for sale – for example, a one-size-fits-all share price

valuation that disregards the size of the package of shares being put up for sale.

- **Notification:** What is the process by which other shareholders are notified? Are there restrictions to the order in which shares are offered? For example, it might be required that the shares are offered to existing shareholders first, then to wider family. There are likely to be details regarding what happens if there are more bids than the shares available. And finally, there is likely to be provision for the eventuality that no bids are received for the shares, including provision for the company to buy back its own shares.
- **Acquirer's undertaking:** Must the seller procure an undertaking from the acquirer that they will join the shareholders' agreement?
- **Thresholds:** For some families with well-diversified shareholdings, there may be rules to prevent a member of the family acquiring shares above a certain threshold or acquiring a controlling interest. Where a threshold is reached, an offer to all shareholders may be required.
- **Gifting:** Gifting of shares may be allowed subject to shareholding limits not being breached, and the recipient being an 'allowable' shareholder.

- **Buy-back provisions:** Where there is either an obligation or procedure under which the company is required to buy back shares in itself, detailed procedures are likely to be in place, including the extent to which the company should build reserves and liquidity for this purpose.
- **Post-disposal protection:** The shareholders' agreement is likely to contain provisions that deal with protection of the company's interests after a disposal. These might include confidentiality or non-compete clauses.

Business valuation and discount on the value of the shares: While the next section deals with the issue of how the business may be valued in more detail, it is worth noting here that it can be very helpful for a shareholders' agreement to contain clauses setting out the basis upon which valuation of shares in the company will be made. Provision can also be made for any discounts that are to be applied to the value of the shares in the event that one shareholder, on wishing to exit the business, sells to the other shareholders.

Dispute resolution: The shareholders' agreement may set out the provisions for what happens in the event of disputes between shareholders, in particular the mechanism by which they will be resolved – arbitration and mediation are two such mechanisms.

5.3 Valuation and discount

a. Introduction

While the intention of the shareholders of the family company is likely to be for the long-term development of the family enterprise, it is both helpful and sensible to develop an understanding or agreement about how shares in the company will be valued in the event that a shareholder wishes to sell his or her shareholding.

An approach by a family shareholder to sell their shares may, in many senses, be unwelcome. An offer by one shareholder to acquire the holding of another may assist the family in keeping the number of shareholders to a reasonable number, but may also be seen as an unhealthy desire to build a more powerful level of shareholding. An agreed approach on how to value the shares in such circumstances is likely to cause much less disruption, both financial and emotional, than the alternative.

The approach to this topic inevitably has to start with an understanding of how to value the shares of a private company, but it should also reflect the family's vision and intention for the family business, as well as the means within the family or the business to fund share transactions.

b. Philosophies and approaches

The previous section on shareholders' agreements looked at the processes by which a transfer of shares can take place, including any limits on the acquisition of shares that may prevent the over-consolidation of shareholdings.

This section looks solely at how shares that may be the subject of a transaction between the owners are valued. The starting point is that, as a 100% family-owned business, there is no market for the shares, so in effect an internal market has to be created. One element in the creation of such an internal market is likely to be that of willing buyer/willing seller.

A number of thoughts are explored below to highlight some of the key issues that can arise.

Type of share: In the majority of scenarios the type of shares being transacted will be ordinary shares with the standard rights attached. It is, however, worth being clear about share type as private companies also issue preference shares and different classes of ordinary share, often with a lettered class designation, eg, A, B or C shares.

Preference shares often have an entitlement to a return, but are normally redeemable at par. They may rank ahead of ordinary shares in a winding-up. A, B or C shares will normally have restricted rights as compared to ordinary shares, perhaps in relation to voting, distributions or the sale of the company.

Valuation of shares in a private company: In relation to ordinary shares, there are a number of methodologies that can be used to value the shares of a private company, including earnings, asset value, dividend yield or an industry-specific valuation methodology. Market practice for the business sector in which the company operates is likely to be as good an indicator as any of which is the most appropriate. Regardless of the methodology, it will be necessary to draw together the appropriate supporting evidence, whether at company or industry level.

Size of holding: Unlike the situation for shares in companies quoted on an exchange, the value attached to a given parcel of shares in a private company is rarely arrived at by dividing the overall value of the company on a *pro rata* basis.

It is quite common for a discount to be associated with minority holdings in a company, as a minority stake, as well as having a general lack of marketability, is likely to have restricted influence in the affairs of the company. Conversely, a strong majority stake, particularly where allied to control of the company, can bring about a premium.

A minority shareholder is one where the level of the shareholding is less than 50%. Below this level, the 25% ownership threshold has some importance as it provides the ability to block extraordinary or special resolutions, whereas holders of less than 25% have little or no control over the affairs of the business.

A majority owner will own more than 50% of the shares, at which level they will be able to pass ordinary resolutions, for example, appointment and removal of directors. Where a majority owner holds more than 75% of the shares, this triggers even greater control as it allows the holder to pass extraordinary or special resolutions altering the company's business, constitution and affairs.

One further complication relates to the number and distribution of holdings of shares in a company. A situation where there is a single majority owner with the remaining shares split across quite a wide number of small holdings is quite different from a situation where there are two 50% shareholdings.

Over and above the natural powers that tend to come with given levels of shareholding, any shareholders' agreement should be checked to see whether any additional powers or restrictions are attached to a given level of holding or type of share.

There is absolutely no hard and fast guide to the level of discount that might apply, and all situations should be taken on their merit. However the ranges in Table 11 give an indication of levels of discount.

Table 11. Levels of discount

<10%	>60% discount
10–25%	40–50% discount
25–50%	30–40% discount
>50%	5–10% discount to a small premium for effective control

'All in it together': The situation in a family company can be different to a situation where two or more unrelated parties are in business together. The ethos in family companies can be described as 'all in it together' and as such the approach to the value of the shares is likely to be 'one price fits all'. That's not to say that a discount couldn't apply, just that any discount would be applied consistently across all shareholders, regardless of the size of the holding.

Discounts can be used to try to ensure that the principle of fairness cuts both ways – that the interests of the shareholders who remain are balanced against the interests of those seeking to leave.

The level of discount can also be used to try to find a fair value per share as the mechanism for balancing the interests of holders of larger blocks of shares with those of smaller blocks.

KEY POINT
The preceding sections set out how the two topics – basis of valuation and level of discount – might be tackled. It will almost certainly be worthwhile seeking external assistance to arrive at a sensible approach for the family.

6. Trust governance elements

6.1 Introduction

From a governance perspective there is a major difference between trust-based inter-generational wealth structures and corporate-based structures.[40] In creating a trust, the person establishing the trust (the settlor) passes title in the assets to a trustee, who then holds those assets for the benefit of one or more beneficiaries subject to the provisions contained within the governing document for the trust – the trust deed.[41] In a corporate-based structure, ownership is typically maintained on a direct basis and when passed from one party or generation to another, title passes absolutely.

This core difference means that the governance elements relating to trusts deserve a separate section, even though many of the considerations relating to surplus and inter-generational wealth transfer remain similar whether a trust-based or corporate-based solution is being contemplated.

In this regard it is crucial that the wealth philosophy of the family – the point and purpose of the wealth – remains central to the governance arrangements put in place for the trust. This should be reflected in the objects set out in the trust deed and in the way the relationships between the parties to the trust, and the wealth it contains, are set out.

In particular, consideration of the effects of the presence of an additional and different relationship – that with the trustee – is crucial given the importance of trust (in the wider sense), communication and next-generation development in the management and passing on of surplus wealth.

The nature, motivation and articulation of a movement of surplus wealth into a trust, and the tone and setting of the relationships that exist in the establishment of that trust, are critical to what happens thereafter. For a testamentary trust this is important, as the settlor will no longer be alive. For *inter vivos* trusts, there can be a tendency for a lesser degree of clarity.

The subsequent development and performance of those relationships in the ongoing running of a trust will undoubtedly influence what happens during the period of a trust's existence, but they won't necessarily be able to make up for what happens at the outset. For good or bad, trustees risk being labelled by beneficiaries as agents of the settlor's preoccupations.

I would highlight a number of potentially troubling scenarios:

Conditional gifts: Surplus wealth gifted into trust in a highly conditional manner, often as a result of wider concerns held by the settlor generation or perceived difficulties regarding the next generation, can see these issues embedded in the trust relationship. Reactions to a controlling parental impulse – whether passivity or even active resistance – are unlikely to be a good foundation for a trust relationship.

Wide discretion: Lack of detailed thought or articulation regarding the purpose of a trust and distributions made from it can lead to discretionary trusts being settled where trustees have wide discretion regarding distributions to beneficiaries. Such situations can be troubling for beneficiaries who, lacking an understanding of what the trust is for, may struggle to build a meaningful relationship with the trustee.

Limited horizons: All too often, the focus is on the here and now, or what's in view – typically the next generation and possibly the one after that. What is often missed is the longer-term view – how things set up today will affect the lives of the third, fourth, fifth or subsequent generations of beneficiaries who will not be known or understood by the settlor, and who in turn won't know or understand why the settlor did what he or she did.

In many cases trust-based structures, with the separation of legal title from benefit, are used to provide protection of the assets from their direct ownership by the individuals who, in the presence of a trust, become the beneficiaries. This protection-based underpinning can lead to numerous issues in relation to the management of and attitude

"Recognising, understanding and dealing with the separation of ownership from benefit, and the creation of the different roles that this implies, is absolutely critical, and should be fully thought through before a trust-based structure is set up."

to the wealth in subsequent generations. In fact, at its worst, it can instil behaviours that act against the development of trust, communication and next-generation development.

That's not to say to say that protective provisions don't have a role; simply that, where possible, they should be balanced by and in support of the positive purpose that the family's wealth philosophy articulates.

Recognising, understanding and dealing with the separation of ownership from benefit, and the creation of the different roles that this implies, is absolutely critical, and should be fully thought through before a trust-based structure is set up. While for many families this separation provides comfort and protection, for many others the deemed loss of control is not something they are willing to contemplate – for such families, a trust-based structure will not be appropriate.

The final point to make in this introduction is the potentially long-term nature of trusts as an ownership structure for wealth. The trust period set for the trust will define this. As trusts can and do last for generations, the implications need to be considered carefully.

In summary, the following are worth reflection:

- the 'voice' of the settlor is articulated in the trust documentation while the settlor is alive, but also when the settlor has passed away;
- the letter of wishes and terms of the trust deed will guide potentially many trustees over many decades and generations;
- while ownership doesn't change, beneficiaries do;
- the nature of the wealth settled into the trust, it's form and future dynamics, and how it is expected to perform over the life of the trust – allowing for the amounts distributed and the potential growth in number of beneficiaries – deserve attention;
- the way in which future, in particular as yet unborn, beneficiaries will relate to the wealth, the settlor(s) and the trustees is a factor in the present;
- an understanding of the role of the trustees – not just their selection, but their ownership structure, succession and replacement – is crucial; and

- the extent of alignment of the trustees' interests with those of the settlor, the beneficiaries and the wealth itself is important.

While it could equally be applied to any form of surplus wealth intended to be passed through the generations, given the nature of trust structures the following stands as a good test to be applied to what is created:

> *It should be our hope that the members of the tribe seven generations from now will honour us for the care and thoughtfulness we exercise in our decision making today.*[42]

Achieving this requires positive action, otherwise natural entropy of purpose, wealth and people will frustrate the good intentions of the owners of surplus wealth.

In the next section we take a look at the governance issues that arise from the perspective of the three main parties to a trust – the settlor, the trustees and the beneficiaries – but also at another role, that of protector, that is sometimes used in relation to a trust.

6.2 Purpose of the trust

Looked at from a governance perspective, purpose can be considered in two parts:

- Why is the settlor motivated to settle a trust?
- To whom and in what way will the trust provide benefit?

The two are linked in that the settlor's motivation will often play out in terms of the way in which the objects are written or expressed; however, the motivation may not be written down. Often it is not even discussed between settlor and beneficiaries, and rarely will it be contained within the trust documentation.

In terms of the relationship between the settlor and the beneficiary, the purpose of the trust is very important as it describes the terms on which the wealth of the settlor is being transferred and made available to the beneficiaries, and it also sets the terms on which the trustees will act, and from which they are unable to depart.

a. Settlor motivation

One of the issues that I see regularly with regard to the establishment of trusts is that of the balance between the positive benefit (or outcomes) that the settlor generation would wish to create with their wealth, and the risk of harm that they see arising from that wealth. All too often, protection from the risk of harm becomes the prevailing narrative in relation to the trust – or perhaps it's just that such structures are naturally more attractive to people who see the world in this way.

This can become self-reinforcing when trust settlors don't then build countervailing strategies to deal with the issues. At times it can feel as though one is dealing with the characteristics of dysfunctional financial families again. Some examples of this syndrome are shown in Table 12.

Table 12. Settlor motivation – dangers and countervailing strategies

Behaviour driven by concern	Countervailing strategies
Secrecy regarding the family's wealth or the existence of a trust is driven by fear of disincentivising the next generation or the belief that they will be profligate	Demonstrate positive values towards wealth and the benefits it can bestow. Demonstrate through settlor behaviours the family's vision and values in respect of their wealth.
Restrictive provisions regarding age for access to the wealth	Prepare and train the next generation.
Restrictive access provisions driven by concerns regarding divorce or remarriage	Make clear the vision and purpose of the family's inter-generational wealth transfer and be proactive in dealing with the risks and concerns.

This is not to say that caution regarding the effects of wealth transfer or the creation of protective provisions isn't justified; it absolutely can be, for example in relation to vulnerable or very young children. It's just that there should be a range of compensating strategies or actions to balance out concerns. Their absence can create problems in the future where, as the issues come out into the open, they become a source of conflict between the generations. Where they are exposed and the settlor has already passed away, they can become even more destructive as there is no opportunity to gain insight or understanding as to why they were originally put in place.

One option for dealing with this is to reflect on what provisions to build into the trust deed (which in general terms may be difficult to amend) or what to put in a letter of wishes (which can be amended as often as is required during the life of the settlor) as guidance to the trustees. This approach allows guidance to the trustees, subject to the limitations of the power to amend the trust deed, to be amended over time in line with the development of the beneficiaries.

b. Objects of a trust

The objects of a trust will be set out in the trust deed and supplemented by a letter of wishes written by the settlor to provide additional, non-binding, guidance regarding his or her intentions.

Because these two documents will articulate the settlor's intentions it's important that they accurately reflect them. And as the intentions have to be formalised in a legal document that either is, or may become, irrevocable, and that may provide discretion to the trustees appointed by the settlor, it's absolutely critical that the following issues are adequately resolved:

- **Settlor self-awareness:** Ideally, the settlor's actions in setting up a trust-based structure for the management and transfer of their surplus wealth will be underpinned by strong and fully reconciled self-awareness. This should be a reflection of the settlor's goals in respect of their non-financial wealth – their wishes for their legacy, for future family relationships, for their reputation and social capital – as well as a reflection of the meaning and purpose of their financial wealth. Sharing this through the documentation underpinning a trust can really help the beneficiaries and trustees to understand the positive purpose behind the settlor's act.

- **Values regarding the family and its wealth:** The settlor should ideally arrive at this point with a strong understanding of his or her family values. Whatever trust structure is put in place, together with the people who will operate it, the family values should be fully reflected. The stronger the articulation of these values in the trust structure, the greater the likelihood that they will be sustained. And this means in the actions of the parties to the trust, not just in the written words of the trust documentation.
- **Intentions for the surplus wealth:** With regard to the wealth within the trust and distributions from it, there are a number of questions to consider:
  - How are the benefits arising to be split between beneficiaries – equally or according to circumstance?
  - How are the benefits to be split between the current and future generations?
  - What distribution purposes are listed? Is it standard wording such as 'maintenance, education or other benefit' or 'health, education, support and maintenance', or are specific purposes listed – maintenance of lifestyle in certain situations; international travel; housing; education; hardship; illness or incapacitation; support for careers or new business ventures; or philanthropy. The somewhat vague catchall, 'other benefit', is a real concern.
  - What is the investment strategy for the assets held?

I would make one final comment regarding the purpose of a trust. Most of this section has looked at the issue of purpose through the eyes of the settlor. But before signing off on the purpose, the settlor should take the opportunity to stand in the shoes of the beneficiary, look back at what he or she has drafted and ask the following questions:

- Do I have a clear understanding why I settled this trust?
- Am I clear about what purpose this trust serves in my life?
- What feelings do I get when I reflect on what this trust means to me?

The same exercise might be repeated in respect of the intended trustees, who might ask the following questions:

- Do I understand the family wealth philosophy and values?
- Has the settlor adequately made clear their intentions? Are they capable of being interpreted and acted on, now and into the future, by me and future trustees?
- Do I believe that the beneficiaries will understand the philosophy and values of the settlor?
- Will I be supported in building an enduring and positive relationship with the beneficiaries?

If the answers aren't positive, further reflection is almost certainly required.

6.3 Parties to a trust

Looking at the parties to a trust through a governance lens will help us to further articulate the challenges and opportunities that arise.

It's crucial to remember that 'parties' are people. Consequently, while we will explore the functions that they carry out in their roles, in the case of trusts it's just as important, if not more so, to understand and appreciate the way in which they perform those roles. We have highlighted the importance of trust, communication and next-generation preparation many times in this book. We should remind ourselves of their continuing importance as we consider the roles played by the parties to a trust.

In thinking through the parties and how the trust is to be organised, it is worth recognising the powers and responsibilities that different parties have, whether conflicts of interest arise from their position, powers or responsibilities, and what checks and balances are put in place to keep these under review.

a. Settlor

The settlor (who may also be known as grantor, creator or trustor) is the person giving the assets. In settling the trust the settlor determines the following:

- what assets are transferred to the trust;

- how the assets in the trust will be used;
- who the beneficiaries will be;
- who the trustees will be, what powers they will have and the basis for their remuneration;
- whether there will be a protector;
- what powers the settlor decides to reserve to him/herself, his successor, or the protector; and
- how long the trust will last.

Trust law requires that there are three certainties in settling a trust:

- **Certainty of object:** the beneficiaries of the trust are made clear.
- **Certainty of subject matter:** identifiable property is being settled into trust.
- **Certainty of intention:** there is a clear intention to establish a trust.

A final thought for settlors, not one often found in the guidance, is to assess the structure for potential conflicts of interest, and to provide measures that enable them to be mitigated or dealt with.

As we indicated earlier, the settlor's intentions will be articulated in the trust deed and in a letter of wishes.[43] Beyond the formal settlement of the trust, the settlor has no formal ongoing role unless he or she reserves certain powers or is one of the protectors or the only protector. Therefore, the way things are set up at the outset will have long-lasting consequences.

b. Trustee

The trustees are the legal owners of the assets held in a trust. They have a number of duties and responsibilities:

- **Administration:** Trustees are responsible for the management of the assets owned by the trust. This will include preparation and maintenance of records, including financial accounts and tax returns; communicating with beneficiaries; and providing them with the information about the trust they require to the extent permitted under the proper law of the trust.
- **Investing:** Assuming the settlor has not reserved this power,

"Trustees have a fiduciary duty to the beneficiaries, meaning they have to act at all times in the best interests of the beneficiaries, to whom they owe this duty of care."

trustees have a responsibility to invest with care and prudence, with a suitable level of risk and diversification, in the interests of the beneficiaries.

- **Distribution:** Trustees have a responsibility to make distributions to beneficiaries in line with the trust. The letter of wishes will guide the trustees in this respect. In some cases this requirement will be explicit within the trust deed – for example, when a beneficiary reaches a certain age. However, usually trust deeds provide trustees with discretion regarding distributions.

  Trustees have a fiduciary duty to the beneficiaries, meaning they have to act at all times in the best interests of the beneficiaries, to whom they owe this duty of care.

  Trustees must not personally benefit from their role, and even trustee remuneration must be specifically authorised in the trust deed.

c. Beneficiary

Whether it's the term 'trust fund baby' or the stereotypical view that the beneficiary of a trust fund is someone with a lot of money and no responsibility, or just the simple fact of appearing to receive something for nothing, the perception of trust beneficiaries often contains references to privilege or being spoiled.

This might make fun headlines in newspapers or magazines, but it is anything but fun should it start to permeate the thinking or actions of those setting up or running a trust. Every effort should be made to develop the recipients of the benefits of a trust into responsible individuals.

That's not to say that the trust deed can't legitimately place limits on the beneficiary's access to the benefits of the trust (for example, age limits, provisions for beneficiaries with special needs or a requirement for pre-nuptial contracts). In fact, it reinforces the need to invest in beneficiary support, education and preparation. Investing in the next generation of beneficiaries should mean building responsibility and accountability from an early age, well before the beneficiaries become aware of the existence of the trust.

Responsibility for this lies with the settlor and the generations of beneficiaries that follow. Each has a duty, in my mind, to prepare the next generation.

These are some of the key matters that a well-prepared beneficiary should have access to and understand:

- the terms of the trust deed;
- the purpose of the trust;
- what the trustee is required to do with the trust capital and income;
- how and why the assets of the trust are invested;
- in what way the beneficiary, or other beneficiaries, may benefit from the trust, and what factors will be taken into account in the making of such decisions;
- the trustee's powers, role and responsibilities;
- any powers conferred on the protector and the rights of beneficiaries;
- the identity of the trustees, the protector (if there is one) and any advisers to the trustees;
- provision for regular meetings with the trustees to discuss the beneficiary's personal and financial circumstances and objectives;
- a general understanding of trust law and accounting; and
- the budgeted and actual costs of running the trust, including the remuneration or compensation paid to trustees.

d. Protector

At its heart, the role of a protector is, as the name suggests, to watch over the trustee and ensure that they act in line with the trust deed and the terms of their appointment. They perform this role through the powers that they are given by the trust deed.

Their role is different from that of a settlor or a trustee, and they can be in a number of forms. A protector can be an individual, a committee or a corporation; a professional protector, family member, close family friend or trusted adviser.

A protector can have powers that might be deemed positive or negative. Positive powers would include matters where the protector is positively empowered to take action:

- removal or appointment of new trustees;
- appointment and removal of beneficiaries; or
- provision of advice to trustees on certain matters such as the appointment of third-party advisers to the trust.

Negative powers cover matters where the protector's consent is required before the trustees can act, perhaps in relation to specific powers or actions:

- the power to appoint and remove beneficiaries or trustees;
- the requirement to seek the protector's consent to the sale, disposal or management of specific assets; or
- the requirement for the trustees to seek the protector's advice or direction in relation to certain matters.

While the appointment of a protector might be seen as offering additional safeguards in relation to a trust, careful thought is required ahead of their appointment as to the definition of their powers. A number of issues, beyond the initial selection of a suitable protector, will need to be considered:

- protector succession or replacement;
- remuneration, and whether to remunerate family member protectors;
- formalities regarding protector actions and involvement, including any liability for their actions;
- the potential for conflicts of interest; and
- an assessment of what might go wrong in the appointment of a protector.

e. Trust advisory committee

Advisory committees are constituted to offer advice to the trustees or to bring the parties to the trust closer together. They do not take decisions – decision making rests with the trustees, and the need for advisory committees is dependent on the nature of the trustees. For example, professional or institutional trustees may be less likely to get to know the beneficiaries, or individual trustees may lack depth of expertise in the fields of investment or philanthropy – in these cases an advisory committee might provide invaluable support and assistance.

Where advisory committees are to be included in the governance of a trust, thought should be given to the articulation of the provision for such bodies. This might include the committee's purpose and goals, or it might set out the access to people and information expected. It might set out the size of the committee, terms of office, meeting schedule, powers and duties.

Examples of advisory committees are as follows:

- **Investment advisory committee:** An investment advisory committee might comprise individuals bringing greater, in-depth experience in those areas in which the trust invests. Where an operating business is held within the trust, it would be important for trustees to have access to individuals with an understanding of the industry in which the business operates.
- **Distribution committee:** A distribution committee might be formed with the role of providing trustees with information to assist them in making distributions from the trust. The important element here is that the distribution committee is charged with developing knowledge of the beneficiaries.
- **Beneficiary education committee:** A beneficiary education committee would be formed to look at how to develop engaged, knowledgeable and purposeful beneficiaries. This would assist beneficiaries in building an understanding of the trust, the role of trustees and how the trust is there to support them, all in a way that builds active participation rather than a dependent relationship between the beneficiary and the trustee.
- **Philanthropy advisory committee:** A philanthropy advisory committee might be established to provide trustees with additional subject-matter support or expertise in assessing philanthropic activity, particularly where the philanthropy is complex in nature. Alternatively, an advisory committee on philanthropy might be used to access a wider set of views or thoughts on the focus of the trust's philanthropy, for example family members or the next generation.

6.4 Types of trustee

A critical decision for the settlor of a trust is the choice of trustee. This involves not just the type of trustee, but the qualities of actual individuals who will fill the role. And of course, given the long-term nature of trusts, the choice is going to have long-term implications, so the issue of trustee succession also has to be considered.

a. Individuals as trustees

Individuals can serve as trustees. For some settlors there is a desire to have someone acting as trustee that they know or trust, and this may be someone close to or a member of the family, or it may be a professional person they know.

Issues to be considered when appointing individual trustees include:

- the number appointed;
- their knowledge, skills and expertise in acting as trustees and managing trusts;
- their knowledge of the settlor's intentions and of the beneficiaries;
- what happens if something goes wrong and action needs to be taken by or against a trustee;
- personal liability of the trustees;
- proximity risk, which may arise from the individual being too close to or at risk of influence by family members;
- succession of the individual trustees;
- cost and remuneration; and
- taxation implications and considerations.

b. Independent corporate trustees

Corporate trustees, according to my definition, are companies that exist solely to act as trustee, although it will be the directors and staff of the company that undertake the activities of the corporate trustee. Corporate trustees offer certain advantages:

- Trustee succession is less of an issue, in that if an individual working with a trust changes, the overall trustee relationship with the corporate trustee doesn't need to change.
- The corporate nature of the trustee provides limited liability protection for the individuals.

- Companies providing specialist corporate trustee services are likely to have built up considerable expertise across a wide range of trust management matters.

The appointment of a corporate trustee does, however, give rise to a number of potential issues that need to be considered. These mainly arise from the fact that the corporate trustee is a separate business with its own corporate objectives alongside the fiduciary duties owed to the beneficiaries. Issues might include the following:

- how to build the right relationships with directors and employees of a corporate trustee, and take account of the risk of staff succession within the corporate trustee;
- understanding how exactly the trustee services work and the levels and scope of service provided, and whether these will adequately meet the requirements of the settlor in creating the trust;
- what happens if something goes wrong;
- cost levels and who exactly has control of the level of costs incurred, now and into the future;
- how a corporate trustee can be replaced;
- whether a sole corporate trustee should be appointed; and
- the location of the trustee and whether the jurisdiction is well regulated.

There is an additional category of trustee under this heading, what we might term an institutional trustee. Institutional trustees will also be companies providing corporate trustee services, but rather than doing this on a dedicated basis, they will provide this alongside other services. A good example of this would be the trust department of a bank. Such organisations will pose many of the same benefits and issues for consideration; however, being larger organisations they may seem more attractive for trusts containing significant assets.

c. Private trust companies

Private trust companies (PTCs) are in fact corporate trust companies but focused solely on acting as trustee for the trust(s) of one family. There is therefore a tendency for them to be used to bring greater control, together with the benefits of having a corporate trustee, while overcoming many of the disadvantages of having individual trustees.

As a company, a PTC will itself need to have an ownership structure. Generally the shares of the PTC will be held through a purpose trust or foundation rather than directly by one or more family members, as this enables ownership to be maintained within the purpose trust or foundation rather than needing to be passed on following the death of a shareholder.

In establishing a PTC a greater level of control can be gained covering some or all of the following areas, and this may provide greater privacy:

- appointments of directors to the board of the PTC, with the opportunity to build succession plans to embed 'institutional memory';
- the policies and procedures, and the structure, of the organisation;
- potentially, decision making for certain specific matters;
- involvement in investment management activities, and other activities such as philanthropy;
- engagement of third-party advisers;
- beneficiary development activities and wider next-generation family member involvement; and
- costs.

Care does, however, need to be exercised in assessing the potential use of a PTC. A clear governance outline needs to be established, with appropriate checks and balances and adequate involvement of independent individuals, as family involvement can lead to conflicts of interest and even family conflict. While control of costs is an advantage, the level of cost in setting up and running a PTC should be assessed. And then there needs to be an assessment of what can go wrong – the consequences and any recourse available. Finally, the features and requirements of the jurisdiction in which the PTC is to be established (for example in the areas of regulation, reporting and taxation) need to be considered, as does the jurisdiction's location proximity to the family.

KEY POINTS

Setting up a trust sees a number of different parties, each with their separate duties and responsibilities, being involved in the management of the settled assets. From a governance perspective, how these roles interact and how the individuals holding the positions then work together is critically important.

Individuals face known or predictable consequences arising from what's set out in the trust deed and their own roles, but they also face unknown and unpredictable consequences in relation to future generations, their lives and attitudes, and future circumstances.

Getting to grips with the governance implications of a trust requires some hard thinking, including consideration of the following areas in anticipation of a discussion of the key technical and legal points relating to the settlement of a trust.

A trust as a vehicle for inter-generational wealth: There are a number of features of trusts that need to be fully grasped and understood. One of the core tenets of a trust is the separation of legal ownership from beneficial entitlement. A second is the tri-partite relationship between settlor, trustee and beneficiary, each having different rights and responsibilities. But equally, developments in the legal and regulatory frameworks for trusts have allowed a degree of flexibility in the way trust arrangements can be created. This complex web of what is and is not possible should be studied carefully and the implications of the route chosen well understood.

Clarity of wealth purpose: As a trust can be a very long-term, even perpetual, instrument, a clear rationale and clear objectives for the wealth settled into the trust need to be established. The trust deed wording should reflect this clearly as there may be very little or even no scope for change (depending on how it is drafted), with only interpretation or discretion providing room for changing circumstances to be taken into account. The motivations of the settlor should be closely examined and, where necessary, subject to robust discussion and challenge before being documented. Does the ensuing trust deed articulate a sense of growth or a sense of control by the settlor? Does the trust deed promote a sense of positivity or protection? Will it generate beneficiary independence or dependency?

Maintaining the family values and wealth: Communication and community within the family, with a view to maintaining and renewing the ethos and values of the family and its wealth, as well as developing the skills, experience and enterprise of future family members, are critical to the healthy functioning of a family and its wealth, regardless of the structure within which the wealth is held and managed. For these reasons, governance arrangements of trust-based structures should include consideration of creating a family council and/or family assembly.

Trustee identification and development: The type of trustee to be appointed should be considered carefully and thoughtfully, and a decision reached that will be appropriate for the near and longer terms. The terms and nature of the relationship to be established should be reflected on, together with review and termination mechanisms. Possible areas of conflict and conflicts of interest should be assessed and appropriate checks and balances introduced wherever possible.

Trustee performance needs to be monitored and kept under review to ensure an appropriate relationship between trustees and beneficiaries, and adequate performance of duties. Future trustees, in whatever form, need to identified, selected and trained. Governance arrangements should make provision for regular meetings and reporting between the parties to the trust, as well as periodic external review.

Beneficiary development: A key aim should be to minimise future beneficiary dependency while maximising beneficiary understanding of the family wealth philosophy and values, of the trust, the opportunities it provides, and future family roles. Governance arrangements might include beneficiary support and a beneficiary development programme. In due course, generations of beneficiaries might well overlap, so how they grow and develop is likely to set the course for the future. The aim is to avoid beneficiary dependency or, put another way, to build beneficiary independence.

Relationship between settlor, trustees and beneficiaries: While the intentions and wishes of the settlor will need to be transmitted to the beneficiaries, great care needs to be taken over how these are expressed. Beyond this, though, trustees need to get to really know and understand the beneficiaries. Governance arrangements should focus on this relationship and how trustees can better understand the lives of the beneficiaries.

A final word

This book is about dealing with surplus wealth.

At the heart of this needs to be the recognition that surplus wealth, as I define it here, is wealth you can't consume yourself – it can only be passed on or given away. Putting the £ and $ signs to one side, it should be relatively easy to become comfortable with this concept. Once it is accepted, preparation for the future and transitioning of the surplus wealth can be dealt with more easily.

I have articulated three important matters that need to be considered – purpose, people and process. *Primus inter pares* is the middle one: people. It is from people that the complexity most often arises. And it is from the complexity around people that the need for governance arises.

Natural governance can only take you so far. If the natural governance that exists in your affairs can sustain you in dealing with your surplus wealth, I would say you are most fortunate, for it is quite likely that the level of complexity inherent in having surplus wealth will require order and planned, rather than natural, governance in both people and process for your purpose to be achieved.

Successful transition of surplus wealth starts with the self-understanding and self-preparation of the transferor or giver. It then moves on to the preparation of the recipients or transferees. Clear purpose and process should then assist in increasing the likelihood of successful transition.

This, to me, is what lies at the core of Seneca's words:[44]

Wealth is the slave of a wise man. The master of a fool.

Notes

1 Consumption here refers to the expenditure of wealth for which there is no return or exchange of financial value – the purchase of another asset is not consumption, while depreciation in the value of the purchased asset would be.
2 "How Many Millionaires Are There In America?", DQYDJ blog post, September 2020. Available at: https://dqydj.com/how-many-millionaires-decamillionaires-america/.
3 Currently defined as those with net investable assets of US$30m or more.
4 See the Global Wealth Sizing Model in *The Wealth Report: The Global Perspective on Prime Property and Investment*, Knight Frank, 2020, p18.
5 Wealth-X, *The World Ultra Wealth Report 2019*. Available at: www.wealthx.com/report/world-ultra-wealth-report-2019/#downloadform.
6 The film *Brewster's Millions* (Silver Pictures, 1985) showed how true consumption, as opposed to spending, of surplus wealth is not easy ...
7 Roy Williams and Vic Preisser, *Preparing Heirs: Five Steps to a Successful Transition of Family Wealth and Values*, Robert Reed Publishers, 2002.
8 *Ibid.*
9 IFB Research Foundation, *Building Family Governance*, Institute for Family Business, 2019. Available at: www.ifb.org.uk/media/4042/building-family-governance-web.pdf.
10 Adapted from IFB Research Foundation, *Building Family Governance, supra*; and Harry F Martin, "Is Family Business an Oxymoron?", *Family Business Review*, June 2001, vol 14 no 2, pp91–96.
11 *Ibid.*
12 Basem A Al-Ubaidi, "Cost of Growing up in a Dysfunctional Family", *Journal of Family Medicine and Disease Prevention*, vol 3 no 3, July 2017.
13 *Ibid.*
14 Gladys Hunt, *Honey for a Child's Heart: The Imaginative Use of Books in Family Life*, Zondervan, 2002.
15 Basem A Al-Ubaidi, "Cost of Growing up in a Dysfunctional Family", *supra.*
16 *Ibid.*
17 See Gerry Johnson, Kevan Scholes and Richard Whittington, *Exploring Corporate Strategy* (7th ed), Pearson College Division, 2005.
18 IFB Research Foundation, *Building Family Governance, supra.*
19 This calculation assumes two children per couple, and that the founders are no longer alive.
20 In this context the term does not refer to the specific legal entity that exists in a number of jurisdictions; rather, it is used generically and the underlying entity may be a trust, company, hybrid or other entity.
21 *Practical Guide to Corporate Governance: Experiences from the Latin American Circle*, International Finance Corporation, Organisation for Economic Co-operation and Development and Global Corporate Governance Forum, 2009. Available at: www.oecd.org/daf/ca/corporategovernanceprinciples/43653645.pdf.
22 The list is paraphrased from the guidance on audit committees on the ICAEW website. Available at: www.icaew.com/technical/corporate-governance/committees/audit-committees/audit-committees-icaew-guidance.
23 The list is paraphrased from ICSA's guidance note, *Terms of reference for the risk committee*, March 2021. Available at: www.icsa.org.uk/my_cg/download-resources/downloadt?fileId=3322.
24 The approach here assumes a joint audit and risk committee, although the considerations would be similar for both committees if they were to be separate.
25 Use of the term 'holding company' is not intended to imply the strict definition of the term as used in corporate governance. For purposes of this book, the term refers to the family business(es) and/or other wealth that falls under its corporate ownership and influence.
26 For the sake of clarity it is worth pointing out that the role of the management board is different from the day-to-day activities of the paid, full-time operational management of the company.
27 *G20/OECD Principles of Corporate Governance*, OECD Publishing, 2015. Available at: https://doi.org/10.1787/9789264236882-en.
28 Although this definition was produced in 1992 by the Cadbury Committee, it is referenced in subsequent versions of the UK Corporate Governance Code (2016 and 2018) and was referred to by the Financial Reporting Council in the 2016 code as the "classic definition".
29 See: Dr Martin Kemp, "Family Business in the UK: The Latest Evidence", IFB Research Foundation online article, September 2020. Available at: www.ifb.org.uk/ifb-research-foundation/articles/family-business-in-the-uk-the-latest-evidence/. The article states that 19.8% of the 1,551 largest businesses in the UK are family owned.
30 *ecoDa Corporate Governance Guidance and Principles for Unlisted Companies in Europe*, European Confederation of Directors' Associations, 2010. Available at: https://ecgi.global/code/ecoda-corporate-governance-guidance-and-principles-unlisted-companies-europe.
31 Didier de Ménonville, KPMG, Paris.
32 Philip Aminoff, president, EFB-GEEF, Finland.
33 ecoDa Corporate Governance Guidance, *supra.*

34 *Ibid.*
35 Available at: www.kodex-fuer-familienunternehmen.de/images/Downloads/Kodex_englisch_2015.pdf.
36 *G20/OECD Principles of Corporate Governance, supra.*
37 *The UK Corporate Governance Code*, Financial Reporting Council (FRC), 2012. Available at: www.frc.org.uk/getattachment/e322c20a-1181-4ac8-a3d3-1fcfbcea7914/UK-Corporate-Governance-Code-(September-2012).pdf.
38 The duties provided are per the UK Companies Act 2006, as they relate to limited liability companies.
39 *Ibid.*
40 This section looks solely at some of the governance implications in the use of trusts in the management of surplus wealth. There are many different types of trust that provide for specific circumstances. This section looks at the topic of trusts in broad terms and specifically does not consider the detailed legal considerations that would need to be contemplated in the use of trusts; nor does it consider the taxation issues. The laws relating to trusts vary between jurisdictions and legal regimes – this section is neither exhaustive in its coverage of topics relating to trusts, nor does it provide any commentary or guidance in relation to any specific type of trust or jurisdiction.
41 The trust deed may be supplemented by a letter of wishes.
42 Attributed to elders of the Iroquois tribe.
43 A letter of wishes outlines to trustees guidance on how the settlor would like trustees to deal with certain aspects of the administration of the trust. It is not binding on trustees and can be changed during the life of the settlor as often as he or she likes. The guidance contained within the letter of wishes can be as detailed or general as the settlor wishes. Letters of wishes are often used where the trust deed provides the trustees with wide discretion.
44 Seneca (5BC–65AD) was a Roman dramatist, philosopher and politician.

About the author

Russell Prior
Consultant and adviser
russell.prior@hsbcpb.com
russellcprior@gmail.com

Russell Prior is an experienced consultant and adviser in family governance, enterprise wealth succession, and family office advisory and philanthropy. He has worked with ultra-high net worth families from across the globe on governance and succession issues regarding surplus wealth.

The core of his work is helping his clients to understand the effects and consequences of the surplus wealth they have, for them and the generations that follow them. Critical to this is achieving harmony, balance and understanding between the purpose, the people and the management processes for their surplus wealth.

His career has spanned corporate banking, wealth management and international philanthropy and he currently leads the family governance, family office advisory and philanthropy practices at HSBC Private Banking, EMEA. He is chair of trustees of two charitable foundations in the UK – Bell Educational Trust Limited and the London Community Foundation. He previously served as a council member of the European Foundation Centre and chair of the UK Finance Hub, and has served as a trustee and non-executive director of a number of charitable organisations. Through this varied experience across different sectors and working with different types of organisation and entity he has seen first-hand the importance of functioning governance systems.

As well as working with families and individuals, he has written numerous articles and spoken at over 130 events on family governance and enterprise succession, as well as advising companies, banks and government agencies on philanthropy. In 2021 he was listed on the *Spears 500* and Citywealth Top Recommended Philanthropic Advisors lists.

About Globe Law and Business

Globe Law and Business was established in 2005. From the very beginning, we set out to create law books which are sufficiently high level to be of real use to the experienced professional, yet still accessible and easy to navigate. Most of our authors are drawn from Magic Circle and other top commercial firms, both in the UK and internationally.

Our titles are carefully produced, with the utmost attention paid to editorial, design and production processes. We hope this results in high-quality publications that are easy to read, and a pleasure to own. Our titles are also available as ebooks, which are compatible with most desktop, laptop and tablet devices. In 2018 we expanded our portfolio to include journals and Special Reports, available both digitally and in hard copy format, and produced to the same high standards as our books.

We'd very much like to hear from you with your thoughts and ideas for improving what we offer. Please do feel free to email me at sian@globelawandbusiness.com with your views.

Sian O'Neill
Managing director
Globe Law and Business
www.globelawandbusiness.com